AFTER PUNISHMENT WHAT?

AFTER PUNISHMENT WHAT?
Discipline and Reconciliation

Parker Rossman

Collins
Cleveland • New York

Published by William Collins Publishers, Inc.
Cleveland • New York

First published 1980

Library of Congress Cataloging in Publication Data

Rossman, Parker, 1919-
   After punishment what?

   Bibliography: p.
   1. Juvenile corrections—United States—Case studies. 2. Juvenile delinquents—United States—Case studies. 3. Juvenile justice, Administration of—United States—Case studies. 4. Punishment—United States—Case studies. I. Title.
HV9104.R66   364.36'0973   79-23738
ISBN   0-529-05734-4

Printed in the United States of America

To Vera Rossman,
compassionate mother
and
to Lou Marsh,
Yale Divinity student
beaten to death by criminals
jealous of his success
in turning youngsters
away from crime

Contents

Preface

AS IN A DETECTIVE STORY we here invite you to reflect upon a mystery: not "who done it" but why American society, which does so many things brilliantly, fails to deter the increasingly serious crimes and criminalization of youngsters like the seven introduced here—interesting teenagers whose crimes and punishments present you with a puzzle.

You must not be sentimental or unrealistic about them, for one may steal your car or rob your home and set it afire while you sleep. If you meet Jimby in court, or in your bedroom at night, you may then be too angry for a reasonable debate about why many people have an uneasy conscience about our juvenile justice system—and the current pressure for harsher punishment of juveniles at a much younger age.

There has been a 1600 per cent increase in juvenile crime in the last twenty-five years and today more crimes are committed by youngsters under fifteen than by adults over twenty-five. Half of the most feared crimes are now committed by juveniles who are acquiring criminal expertise and careers at an early age.

In a time when many feel that society is punishing very poorly, a sampler in a farmhouse kitchen reads:

> . . . a sound tree bears good fruit
> *punish well,*
> you will know them by their fruits.

Our concern with punishing *serious crimes well* rules out a discussion of the delinquencies of nearly all youngsters such as traffic offenses, abuse of alcohol and drugs, truancy from school and home, consenting sexual explorations, trespassing, petty theft,

9

fighting. We define "serious crime" as law-breaking that becomes habitual and leads a youngster into a criminal milieu with adult or professional/criminal associates. Our society is so organized—or disorganized—that petty delinquencies can lead a youngster into a criminal career if he or she gets caught up in the justice system.

Perhaps you have never had the chance to get acquainted personally with youngsters involved in lethal arson, blackmail, extortion, assault, robbery. Nor have many of us even kept records of the punishments inflicted upon our own children at home, at school, on the street. So we know little about the psychological impact, the brooding, the meanings that children may attribute to such experiences.

What do we know about "punishing well" to increase the effectiveness of punishment?

I began these interviews in an effort to help clergy become enablers—to prod church members into working to improve the quality and effectiveness of the services provided to troubled youngsters and families. We set up a field trip to help a clergy group clarify this enabling function, beginning at a state training school where the chaplain selected two teenage inmates for us to study. He helped us meet nearly every adult who had been involved in punishing these two juveniles from the time they first got into trouble, one of them at age six.

Many of the officials we interviewed wanted to join us for the rest of the field trip to see what other professionals would say, for each could add one small piece to the puzzle which was gradually assembled to provide a picture both fascinating and appalling to all adults who had been involved in punishing the two offenders. These professionals had thought that they were involved in "team work" and "coordination of efforts" but found that, in fact, they had treated these two juveniles like hospital patients who received medication from different physicians and nurses, none of whom knew what medicine the others were giving.

"You can kill a patient that way," one social worker said. "I see now that each of us assumed that someone else was giving more attention to diagnosis, to monitoring of treatment. These two youngsters were lucky that most of us did nothing but rattle papers."

Perhaps the clergy on that field trip stumbled accidentally onto cases of benign neglect that were in no way typical. The stories told here were not selected as a scientific sample to use in recommending reforms or drawing responsible conclusions. Our purpose rather is to stimulate more reflection about why punishment alone is not enough to deter such juveniles and to motivate ordinary citizens to play their essential role in juvenile crime prevention. We have changed all names and places, in order to make sure that no one can be recognized and to protect the identity of both youngsters and professionals who were willing to be unusually candid with us.

The seven juveniles described in this book were selected simply because their records were available and it was possible to interview people who had been involved in their punishments. Among these there is only one girl because we could only find one within the limits of these possibilities, and perhaps because boys dominate such serious crimes.

Rather than beginning with a definition of punishment, the first chapters tell the interesting stories of how seven youngsters were punished. The second half of the book then asks what else might have been done to deter their crimes and criminalization—when punishment failed. While the experts debate their theories of retribution, "just deserts," deterrence—books to review such discussion are recommended at the end of the book—ordinary citizens must continue to elect legislators and judges and must make provisional decisions about what to do in the interim with arrested juveniles. Religious people have a special obligation to debate and to experiment with redemptive alternatives—especially for children. We propose here some things that volunteers can do in every community to establish meaningful, reconciling relationships which can help deter crime even while waiting for the experts to determine long-range solutions to juvenile crime.

Niantic, Connecticut   PARKER ROSSMAN
August 15, 1979

Part One

How
Were They Punished?

WE CALL IT MURDER

The citizens of this city were angry when an eighty-year-old woman was paralyzed for life as a result of an attack during an armed robbery and when a young policeman—father of five small children—was shot in the head for no apparent reason. Now another young hood, whose name cannot appear in the newspapers because he is only fifteen, is released on suspended sentence after fourteen serious arrests, two terms in correctional institutions, a kidnapping, car theft, and drunken driving without a license that resulted in the death of a fine teacher and her baby.

We call it murder. He was transporting a minor girl for purposes of prostitution, in a stolen car in which a gun and stolen merchandise were found. We join voice with citizens now demanding action by the legislature to match that of nearby states where such a boy would be tried in adult court with a mandatory prison sentence—in such crimes as kidnapping, armed robbery, or homicide. Who will be to blame now when this boy goes out and kills again?

*From a newspaper
editorial about Jimby*

CHAPTER 1

Punishment
Without Reconciliation

THE OWNER OF A CANDY STORE, his customers harassed by Jimby and his friends who regularly conducted criminal business outside, one day plaintively asked, "Can't anyone do something about those damned kids?"

Jimby's priest, commenting on the boy's punishment said, "If they are damned kids, I ask who has damned them? The damned are those for whom there is no forgiveness, those who are not reconciled after punishment. Damnation is punishment without end."

"The candy-store owner thinks that the solution is more punishment," I said. "That parents, schools, police, and courts have been too lenient, too permissive. Do you think so?"

"The candy store owner was in a Nazi camp as a child so he knows something of damnation. I suppose that's where he got a strong taste for vengeance, wanting to bring the wrath of God down on all those youngsters, save one."

"Jimby?"

The priest laughed. "Jimby has been everyone's favorite, always the charming politician who knows how to bribe us all with a helping hand; in my case by regularly attending mass with his mother and by faithfully confessing his sins."

"Is it true that Jimby organized neighborhood kids to wash off the graffiti?"

The priest nodded. "As voluntary penance, although I doubt if

15

Jimby is a great believer in penance. We somehow raised him to be a sort of Protestant. You see Jimby lives in a state of grace . . ."

"A young pimp, killer, dealer in stolen goods?"

"Maybe it isn't *Christian* grace," the priest replied, "but Jimby accepts some responsibility for his conduct and life and even for his world, whereas his friends are often plagued with feelings of unworthiness, of helplessness, of being victims of society. Of all the young criminals in this neighborhood, Jimby is unique in his strength of character. I can't help respecting a kid who struggles to wriggle out of the trap, to resist the punishment which is imposed to batter him down."

"You demand law and order in your homilies," I asked.

"And punishment for the wicked. How else can there be law—or respect for and enforcement of law? Jimby wonders, however, why he should be punished for theft when the police make little effort to catch the people here who buy stolen goods, who tell their friends where they can get "bargains." After many deliberate crimes, Jimby now faces severe punishment. Will it deter others or save him?"

The juvenile court judge was too busy to talk to me until she found that I wanted to ask her about Jimby. She said, "He needs only three words to persuade you that he is a saint until you see how thick his file is!" She held up Jimby's folder of offenses. "At age fifteen his whole life is up for the toss of a coin. He may well cost the taxpayer a half million dollars in court, police, and prison costs during the next twenty years, unless . . ."

"What is the role of punishment in determining that toss of coin?"

The judge turned to stare out the window. "Am I responsible to him or to society? The public is demanding harsher punishment for boys like Jimby who are guilty of repeated offenses. Legislation is pending which would authorize me to lock him up for five to ten years."

"I suppose I shouldn't ask what you are going to do with him?"

"You may ask," the judge replied, "because I haven't the slightest idea yet. I will be condemned if I send him to jail—or if I let him go and he breaks the law again."

"What about other alternatives? Treatment or therapy programs?"

"They are all fake," she snapped, "even if operated by highly competent, dedicated people, because they are unrealistic about the neighborhoods and families of these youngsters. Last week, for example, we had a boy back on another charge of selling drugs. We had put him through an effective drug dependence program and he was clean, but he went home to a mother who gave him pot to sell because the welfare money had run out. He went home to a street where all of his friends use drugs and where he couldn't find another job. There was nothing wrong with his drug dependence program. He went out rehabilitated—but his family and neighborhood were not."

"You mean a program is fake unless it also treats the family?"

"Yes, family and neighborhood—unless you take the family away or immunize them all."

"Immunize is an interesting word," I said.

"Some kids grow up in vicious neighborhoods and turn out well, and Jimby and his brothers may all end up as good citizens, if society looks the other way while they steal enough money to get out. Society does that much of the time instead of providing jobs for the 40 percent of young people who are unemployed in Jimby's neighborhood. Jimby already shows signs of immunization in that he is sick of crime and wants out."

"Jimby's victim demands revenge for a dead wife and child," I said. "Can you punish him in some way that won't turn him into a criminal mastermind as prison is likely to do?"

The judge turned to look me in the eye. "Off the record, I sometimes think that the wise and humane thing to do would be to give Jimby fifty lashes at the cost of maybe fifty dollars instead of spending $50,000 to $100,000 on imprisonment."

"You're not serious in suggesting a return to torture, barbarism?"

"Is what will happen to Jimby in the reformatory any less barbarous? Is psychological torture so much more humane? Somewhere our society got the unworkable idea that we could punish and rehabilitate at the same time in prison. In fact, rehabilitation can only begin—in most cases—when the punishment is over, and when is that for Jimby? In many cases it would make sense to send a boy to a rough prison for six weeks—after that the trauma begins to wear off as he learns to cope. The shock of a rough six weeks might open him to programs of rehabilitation."

"Such as?"

"I wish I knew. Religious groups ought to experiment with new alternatives. The court can decide upon guilt and can punish but shouldn't someone else then be responsible for treatment and rehabilitation? Most parents know from experience that punishment can simply increase rebellion, resentment, hate, deception, and delinquency unless it is followed by loving forgiveness and the offender is welcomed back into the family circle. Perhaps punishment criminalizes whenever that process is not completed. Whenever I start to lecture a juvenile I always remember what my father said when he punished me: 'This is going to hurt me more than you but I am doing it because I care about you.' My mother was wiser. She knew that love was suspended during punishment, that you can't heal the bruises until after the beating is over."

"You feel that your task, in the justice system, is only to punish, not to rehabilitate?"

"Our knowledge and practice is as primitive as medical science was two centuries ago," the judge replied. "The public demands that I punish harshly or be replaced, but if more punishment would prevent crime, few of these youngsters would ever appear in my court. Far from being raised permissively they have been punished and punished and punished . . . and to what effect?"

Not Either/Or

The social worker who pulled Jimby's records together for me was a hard, tough woman who could have been cast as guard in a concentration camp. She was a veteran of thirty-five years of futile efforts to keep drowning families afloat.

"I think swift, just, fair punishment can deter," she said, "but not as long as 10 per cent of juveniles get caught and only 2 per cent actually end up in court. Odds of 10-2 are good enough to try anything in Jimby's end of town."

"But sooner or later they get caught, don't they? If they keep stealing?"

"It depends on how clever they are and who is protecting and helping them," she replied. "The word on Jimby's street is that he had bad luck, so there won't be much deterrence in his punishment. The problem with 'punishment for deterrence' is that society begins too late. Jimby and his friends were stealing when they were eight years old."

"You feel that parents are too permissive?"

"Not the ones I meet." She stamped her cigarette out angrily.

"Was Jimby disruptive at school?"

"At times, with incompetent teachers who only knew how to punish. But Jimby grew up in a close, supportive, and caring family. Aware that they lived in a jungle, Jimby's brothers taught survival techniques, how to endure pain and punishment, how to take pride in being able to withstand it. They taught him to cope by being tough. Jimby had a punitive teacher in sixth grade who was placed there to impose respect for law and order with a big paddle on a difficult class. The teacher lost control of the class for perhaps the same reason that society seems to have lost control over Jimby's neighborhood. If you place your faith in 'punishment for deterrence,' what do you do when it doesn't work?"

"What will work?"

"Jimby was speeding and Jimby was drinking," she continued. "He is angry with himself for being foolish and stupid, since he is usually clever. Now if he is helped, I think his family and girl friend will see to it that he won't speed again while drinking. Only they can really deter him."

"So it doesn't matter whether Jimby is punished or not?"

"A foolish question since he has already been drastically punished by his own remorse and his family's scorn and shame. The teacher, whose wife and unborn child were killed in Jimby's drunken accident, left his job as lay teacher in a Catholic school to devote his life to helping troubled youngsters and Jimby knows that."

"The dead woman's husband wouldn't speak to me," I said.

"He is ashamed, enraged over what his wife's death has done to his own faith. He told me that he wants Jimby locked up in a harsh, cruel place and that no punishment Jimby could receive from warders or fellow prisoners would be enough. Yet he knows that he sins when he nurses resentment and a desire for revenge. He said to

Jimby, 'How can I forgive until God helps me? How can forgiveness
be a duty?'"

"What did Jimby say?"

"He wept."

Pieces of a Puzzle

A policeman who knows Jimby well was more interested in asking questions than in giving answers. "Punishment? Let me ask you,
how does American society think crimes can be prevented?" He
gave me no chance to answer. "If the family crumbles, the second
line of battle is the church, boys' clubs, scouts and all—and that
line crumbles fast when the heat is on, so society sees cops as the
third line of battle. Right?"

"Most Americans," I suggested, "see cops as the first line."

"Now you're really hitting on target. Society acts as if crime can
be prevented by laws. The kids are drinking or smoking pot so the
legislature passes laws against it and they all stop, right? All the kids
in Jimby's neighborhood steal, so the legislature passes a tougher
law and they stop, right? The country needs to conserve energy so a
law is passed to forbid anyone to drive over 55, so no one does,
right?"

"Laws prevent crimes only when they are enforced," I said.

He laughed. "By more cops on the beat, more schoolguards?"

"I guess that's what people think."

The policeman from Jimby's neighborhood pointed a contemp-
tuous finger at me. "Even in prison there isn't much law and order
except as the convicts cooperate. So how much crime do you think
cops can prevent here on Jimby's street without the active cooperation of a majority of residents?"

"Not much," I agreed. "Does punishment prevent crime?"

"The death penalty? Fines? Prison?"

"I'm asking you."

"Hell, if I knew how to prevent crime I'd get a Nobel prize or
something. Cops here simply gather up the rubbish to dump them
into jails and courts. I may have deterred Jimby some . . ."

"By watching him closely, knowing what he was up to?" I asked.

The policeman thought my remark was hilariously funny. "I
doubt if an army of cops could hamper Jimby's style merely by

surveillance. No, I have some impact on him through man-to-man talks because he likes me and I like him. I admire his self-esteem."

"What do you talk about?"

"Sometimes I just harass his gang. That works. Or I talk to him about his hopes for a home, for good kids who won't need to steal, who will do well in school. These hopes deter him more than anything else, because he loves Francine."

"I want to know who has punished Jimby, and how, and why, and where, and the consequences."

"Ask him," the officer said. "Jimby is the best talker in his part of town!"

One clue to the mystery of failing court punishments can be found in the confusing and different uses of the word "punishment" by parents, social workers, court officials, clergy, youngsters, and others who report the application and interpretation of the meaning of punishment. Before we turn to a definition of punishment in Chapter 9, play the game of noticing the differences between what people *say* about punishment in these case stories and what they actually *do* about it. Psychologists who know how to change a specific behavior by applying a stimulus might hedge their bets by defining punishment as "a stimulus directly applied to an individual with the consequence of probably altering future behavior."

CHAPTER 2

Jimby

"Punishment?" Jimby says, "I'm man enough to take whatever they dish out. I am proud of that."

JIMBY WAS QUITE DIFFERENT in person than the picture I had of him from the newspapers. I found him in a nonalcoholic bar playing chess with his seventeen-year-old brother, Bork, who looked like a juvenile criminal although he never missed school and had an excellent reputation at the supermarket where he worked. Jimby, on the other hand, looked like the boy in the TV commercials: blond, open-faced, the sturdily talented rogue who in 1776 would have shocked his law-abiding neighbors by taking a musket to go fight the king.

Bork was intrigued with the idea of discussing punishment: "When Jimby was three, mom caught him in her purse and slapped his hand. Instead of crying he protested, 'No! You're supposed to keep an eye on me.'"

That phrase was on everyone's lips at Jimby's house, for his mother had taught her children to protect and care for each other.

"We always felt that mom was watching us," Jimby said, "like God, she seemed to know everything we did."

His mother kept close watch from the window of her second-floor apartment above the bar where she worked at night. She was a beautiful girl who had married at seventeen and had lost her teen-age husband through tragic illness two years later. Each of her seven children had a different father and although she was a prostitute, she was respected in the neighborhood for her pride in taking care of herself and her children without welfare.

"She was no street walker, never," Jimby said. "She taught us to take care of ourselves the best way we could and she still hopes to get us out of here to a situation where we can all obey the law and she won't have to be ashamed."

She kept her family together with a warm, enfolding love which was never possessive, inspiring a fierce loyalty in her children to herself and to each other. She was not the only one in the neighborhood, however, who drilled into her children the ambition to get out of the slum into a suburb where they could live honest, decent lives.

The priest said, "Everyone in this area seems to dream of the suburbs much as their grandparents hoped to go to heaven."

"Mom seldom hit us," Bork said. "But our older brothers did. Somehow mom raised us to discipline each other."

Jimby nodded. "I'd rather go to jail any day than be punished by my brothers! I might want to kill a teacher who laid a hand on me, but when Ken, my big brother, ruled that I was out of line I knew that I deserved whatever I got; and anyway, they were teaching me how to take it, how to get along."

"To get along" meant survival training by his older brothers to make Jimby tough enough to take whatever a punishing life might have in store for him. The other brothers belonged to a street gang known as the Ringers ("We wring the necks of the chickens") and they helped Jimby create his own street gang, the Rollers, because at that time the kindergarten crowd all aspired to skate. While the gangs rejected the sissy, the tattle-tale, the continually-sick boy with the runny nose, or the "silent queer" as members, Jimby's brothers insisted that every child who lived on the block had the right to gang protection. That is, residency gave certain territorial rights and the Rollers were obliged to punish any intruders who teased girls or the weaker boys.

Under Jimby's leadership the Rollers had three moral rules of life-and-death importance—

> Be strong enough to take your punishment.
> Be clever and don't get caught.
> Get even with anyone who tries to push you around.

His Punitive Street

"Maybe mom didn't punish us much at home," Bork said, "but we really got it on the street."

Sociologists describe Jimby's neighborhood as a "criminalizing environment" because the citizens turn their eyes aside to ignore each other's illegal activities. It was especially dangerous to notice the activities of juvenile or adult gangs who looted the boxcars on the railroad siding. Retribution was harsh and swift upon anyone who "stuck his nose into someone else's business." Homes might be burned, robbed, or vandalized. "So," Bork explained, "the rule is, you keep your nose out of my cigarette smuggling and I'll not notice when you bribe the building inspector."

For a time the responses to questions about Jimby's punishment were puzzling until it became clear that Jimby was not so much punished as a *punisher*. He was the one who "got even," who retaliated as the instrument of retribution, who believed strongly in punishment-for-deterrence. The "honest thieves" who were simply trying to use crime to assemble enough capital to get out to the suburbs were angered by the addicts and crazies whose irrational crimes drew the attention of the cops.

Jimby once told a priest that God was more likely to answer the prayers of people who lived in the suburbs. When the priest tried to argue the point, ten-year-old Jimby had simply waved his hand at the street and said, "God doesn't seem to be around here very much looking after his children."

That conversation took place shortly after Jimby's most traumatic experience with punishment, which brought his childhood to an end. One night a little girl screamed for help in an alley behind Jimby's home. The neighbors assumed that she was being battered by a drunken parent so one good citizen telephoned the police anonymously, then closed his window to mask the screams, turning up the volume on the stolen radio he had bought from Jimby's older brother, Ken.

The police found a dead child in the alley, not Jimby's eight-year-old sister who had been screaming, but the twelve-year-old feeble-minded boy who had tried to rape her. Jimby's brothers had retaliated as punishers who "did what needed to be done." They felt justified about killing the feeble-minded boy because "he was a menace like a mad dog, terrorizing younger children," and because "the cops and courts would hardly do anything about it at all."

Jimby, who had been memorizing the Ten Commandments at his C.C.D. classes, was sure that the wrath of God would descend upon them and especially upon him for his part in the murder.

"What if we get caught?" he had whispered.

"Then we take our punishment," an older brother said. "An eye for an eye, a tooth for a tooth."

Jimby prepared himself to endure any punishment, but instead of suffering the wrath of God he felt confirmed as a punisher, as an instrument of God's retribution in areas where punishment was otherwise neglected. He was cynical about the police who rounded up every known homosexual (since the murder victim was a boy). One of them, a man who was at the bar with Jimby's mother at the time of the murder, was hounded out of the area, "even though everyone knew he was innocent," Jimby said, "including the cops."

Interpretation of Punishment

"Where was God?" Jimby asked the priest, who replied, "God has no hands on earth but ours. He expects us to do his will."

So Jimby wondered if perhaps God had spared him to help bring justice to the downtrodden, to punish the wrong-doers. He and his gang smashed windows at a drug store where a clerk refused to help a boy who had cut his hand.

"Vandalism?" Jimby said. "There's always a reason around here."

Teachers and court officials who punished Jimby were puzzled by the seeming lack of effect, but perhaps the impact was different than they had wished and expected. From an early age, Jimby was taught by his brothers to experience punishment as a sort of "boot-camp" training in endurance, to be accepted—no matter how painful—with the self-discipline of the martyr or saint who understands suffering as strengthening his spirit, as suffering for the good of all.

Jimby was not in rebellion against his family but has always been intensely devoted and loyal to them, seeing punishment as something that makes sense within the family circle or when a gang punishes one of its own members that it cares about. In that context the experience of painful retribution toughens and strengthens the spirit, where otherwise it is a weapon of war.

When Jimby was arrested the first time, he was taken home by the police because of his young age and his mother promised that he would be punished for breaking the windows. The promise had to be honored so there was a family conference on two important questions: *why* was he to be punished and *how*. Jimby's mother withdrew to the bar and his brothers agreed that the crime for which he had to be punished was "getting caught." He had reasons to "get even" but his stupidity in getting caught was unforgivable. "Was the punishment painful?" I asked.

Jimby grinned sheepishly. "Like when the guys all pile up on you in a football game. If you play the game you have to take the punishment."

His brothers decided to punish Jimby as he might be punished in jail, so he spent the night fighting people who were older, bigger, tougher, more experienced—his brothers. They made him fight for food, for a drink of water, for his clothes, and as he fought each brother that evening, the others coached him on how to attack boys who were older, larger, and stronger. "They call the detention house a 'home,' Bork explained to Jimby. "But if you go there you'll find it is more like a boxing ring."

The next day the policeman who had brought Jimby home came with a paper to be signed, and perhaps to inquire if the promise to punish Jimby was really being carried out. When he saw the boy's black eye, bloody nose, and bruises, the cop simply said, "I didn't mean for you to be that rough on him."

Jimby knows what is right and wrong and his attitude toward the conventional Catholic morality he has been taught at school and church suggests the importance of how a youngster understands and interprets punishment. Jimby feels that he does *not yet* belong to the structures of conventional society, that Christian morality does not yet apply to him, that he can become law-abiding when he moves to a "good suburb." Like a soldier on the battlefield who is removed from the sort of community where it is possible to live without killing, Jimby sees himself as living by an interim morality which allows him to use gun and knife, even to murder a twelve-year-old boy. Jimby does not approve of prostitution, especially that of his mother, but he explains that she had no honorable way to feed her children so—using an explanation common in his home—he said, "You do what you have to do and take the consequences."

Jimby said that God and all decent people condemn prostitution but does not blame the prostitutes, or the pimps who protect them. God, Jimby said, blames the men who come from the suburbs to the bar under his mother's apartment. As for girls in his neighborhood, if they are pretty, poor, not too bright, he sees it almost inevitable that they will succumb to offers of money, adventure, and perhaps a chance to get out of the slum. As a protector, Jimby sees himself as possibly helping such girls find "a rich guy who would marry them and take them out of here."

Jimby's social worker said, "He and his brothers have the reputation of being loyal to their girl friends in a neighborhood where many boys amuse themselves by tricking, deceiving, and seducing girls. And," she added, "it's not Jimby's fault that he isn't married to the mother of his baby. He and Francine would be married if he could get a job."

His judge said, "A boy like Jimby, if he finds a way to marry and support his family, may in the long run be less of a threat to the community than many boys not yet arrested or thought to be criminal."

Jimby recalls his first arrests as involving more adventure than shame or punishment, like going to the dentist for a checkup: "Big people grab you, shake you, tell you what is going to happen to you if you aren't good, then let you go." He laughed. "In this neighborhood a 'good' kid is going to get trampled on by the others." He meant that conventional goodness is almost impossible there without the support of a strong family and friends, which helps explain why teachers, police, and courts often settle for a *promise* 'to be good' rather than for any real change in behavior.

Yet there is another kind of "goodness" that Jimby respects, namely loyalty to friends even if it means defying the court, keeping promises even if it means going to jail. On Jimby's mother's refrigerator is a slogan in crayon: "Don't be good, be the best."

Court Punishment

Jimby's court social worker first met him when he was twelve, after his fifth major offense. "I found him to be somewhat impudent, but my encounter with him brightened an otherwise depressing day. I asked, "Aren't you a bit young to be breaking into boxcars?"

He replied, "You mean it will be OK when I'm older?"

The social worker repressed her smile and replied sternly, "No, I meant you are young for the punishment you deserve."

"I can take it," he replied.

When she said, "You and I have some business to do," she was not ready for his reply.

"Would you like to buy a new color TV set?"

Jimby was not merely being sassy. His brother, Ken, an appliance repairman, was banking every illegal dollar to buy a house for his wife and children. Nearly everyone in the neighborhood appreciated being able to buy appliances at bargain prices and most of them knew perfectly well that such items were not "left unclaimed."

When the social worker scolded Jimby, saying that she would be punished, too, if she bought stolen TV sets, he gravely nodded and said, "Then you think good people should be punished along with the bad?"

She was puzzled by the question until she realized that on Jimby's street the "bad people" stole and the "good people" bought stolen merchandise. Jimby thought *buying* was worse since that made the crime profitable.

He asked, "Is the girl who whores as bad as the john who talks her into it by waving a fifty-dollar bill from his car window?"

The social worker found that Jimby could expound Catholic theories of morality, especially liberation-theology views, that God in Christ sides with the poor against their oppressors."

"Robin Hood?"

"No, he mixes his liberation theology with American capitalist individualism, considering himself personally responsible to get himself out of the slum and into a situation where he can serve justice. To shock him into realizing that his view of American justice was off base, we decided to incarcerate Jimby for a time. He was a boy of such promise that we felt he had to be taken out of his home and neighborhood and sent him to a Catholic protectory."

Jimby did not appreciate the court's effort to put him under church influence and saw the protectory sentence as a shocking punishment, being taken away from his family, friends, and girl. He was prepared for jail but not for affection that challenged him profoundly.

The social worker continued. "I think it might have worked if the protectory had followed court instructions that Jimby not be allowed a weekend at home for at least six months. He was worried, however, about his girl, about debts he owed, and quickly seduced the priests into thinking he had a vocation. Jimby made straight A's, asked for special prayers, and asked to go home for the weekend to talk to his own priest. He was again arrested for breaking into a boxcar while home for the weekend."

"So he had to be punished more severely."

"The fathers were terribly disappointed, felt he had betrayed them, put him into tighter security; but he was able to run away again within a few weeks. The fathers were hurt when Jimby requested a transfer to a reform school. They wanted to give him another chance, but Jimby correctly figured that he might stay in the protectory for years, while he could soon get out of jail on probation. He wasn't fooling me, but he kept running away from the protectory and his behavior was perfect at the training school. Not one fight in three months, probably because he organized others to fight for him just as he organized others to steal for him once he was out. This is often a first step towards a professional career in crime—a really smart kid begins to recruit others to take the risks."

"Then was Jimby ever really punished by the court?"

The social worker nodded. "He was harshly punished, physically and psychologically by the 24-hour-a-day surveillance at the protectory and training school. He was already accustomed to adult freedom, to sleeping at times with his girl, so at thirteen he came out resolved never to be arrested again."

"But not resolved to avoid breaking the law?"

She laughed. "No! More like the truck driver who carefully uses his CB radio to make sure he breaks the speed laws only when no cops are around. But Jimby's long arrest record was over for many months—until he had this accident. Jimby had been drinking at a farewell party for a girl who was going off to live with a businessman who had set her up in an apartment. Everyone had congratulated her for getting away from a stepfather who had been forcing her sexually and who was responsible for her prostitution. Jimby was charged with delivering a prostitute when, in fact, he was trying to help a prostitute move up a notch in life."

"But in a stolen car."

"Her stepfather's car which may actually have belonged to her real father. Again Jimby was doing what seemed necessary out of loyalty to a friend."

"Can Jimby be sent back to the protectory?"

"No, it's closing and the court has fewer options each day for a fifteen-year-old like Jimby with a long record of juvenile offenses. Jimby is very unusual, an intelligent youngster who will probably be able to cope with any punishment. The reformatory may confirm a criminal career, but maybe not, because he loves his girl and he is crazy about his baby."

After long delays, the court sentenced Jimby to three years, with the understanding that he would be released on probation immediately if he would marry Francine, finish high school, and would work four evenings a week in the hospital emergency room.

"I wanted Jimby to talk with his victim's husband, and Jimby was willing," the judge said. "I changed my attitude toward Jimby when I learned that he and Francine had gone to the funeral home during visiting hours to see the woman and baby he had killed. They didn't do it to impress me and I found out about it only by chance. It took great courage on his part to go, because he knew those people were ready to lynch him. I could suspend his sentence with a fairly clear conscience also because I have got a firm commitment from Jimby's mother, his brothers, and from Francine that Jimby will keep his contract with me, and they are an honorable bunch when it comes to keeping their word."

"So he is punished by seeing how people are hurt in accidents like the one he caused," I suggested.

"No!" the judge replied. "I think Jimby can be changed by this chance to help heal people's pain."

Dr. Richard Otto, author of "A Comparison of Positive Reenforcement Punishment in Two Special Education Classes," (University of Connecticut, 1978) told the story of a mother who proposed to punish her son by forbidding him to fish all summer, his main pleasure in life. Otto suggested to her that the punishment might achieve its objective if the privilege was withdrawn only one day at a time, whereas such "over-punishment" would remove the most constructive "positive reenforcement" from the boy's life. The mother, however, insisted on the "harsher punishment" with the result that her son's delinquencies increased all summer. The mother, Otto says, violated the principles of effective punishment as courts so often do.

Jimby's brothers didn't "punish" the feeble-minded boy. They killed him. Similarly many people who strongly believe in punishment *do not know how to make it work.*

Yet nature punishes and effectively changes our behavior immediately when, for example, we touch a hot stove.

MINOR ARRESTED
IN PORNOGRAPHY CASE

A teen-age boy was arrested late yesterday as part of a two-month investigation of child pornography. Emilio S., 16, was apprehended selling "dirty pictures" behind a junior high school, and admitted to police that he had recruited youngsters for pornographic film sessions. He led police to a cache of films in a walk-up apartment on Seventh Street which had been temporarily rented by a man the boy knew only as "Rito." The boy admitted that he had jumped bail in New England while waiting trial on drug charges.

The CHICAGO TRIBUNE News Service reports child pornography to be big business. Authoritative estimates range upward from 100,000 appearing in photographs and films. "Many of the children," according to the TRIBUNE, "are runaways who receive affection and approval from adult exploiters, which they never had in their broken homes." Under new anti-pornography laws, this sixteen-year-old must be tried in adult court and, if guilty, the mandatory sentence will be three to ten years.

Newspaper story about Emilio

CHAPTER 3

Emilio

"I got it coming," Emilio said about his punishment. *"I didn't want to do things. Guess the devil does it in me."*

"WHAT ELSE COULD WE HAVE DONE to save Emilio from hell?" his grandmother asked asked Luiz, the graduate student in sociology, who interviewed members of the arrested boy's family. Emilio's grandmother insisted that everything possible had been done to keep him from crime. His strict Pentecostal parents allowed no TV, movies, or "anything else that might give him bad ideas." He was taken to church seven nights a week from the time he was a baby and was half-grown before he was allowed to go anywhere unchaperoned. He was seriously punished for even the most minor misdeed even before he was old enough to walk.

Luiz found Emilio while tracking down sources of pornography for a research paper. The fifteen-year-old fugitive was living by this trade he loathed, seeing himself sink deeper into a quagmire each day, desperately afraid of prison. Luiz tried to persuade Emilio to turn himself in to the police, offering friendship, help, and an attorney. The boy often talked to Luiz about surrendering but could never bring himself to do so.

Emilio's pastor, who came a great distance to see the boy after his arrest, said, "Emilio seems to think hell is inevitable, because he has only heard his father's preaching, not mine. His father is a stock clerk who seems never to have heard the good news, only the bad."

Even when Emilio was only two and three years old, his father whipped him regularly with the buckle end of a belt for any viola-

35

tion of the sabbath, shouting scripture verses as he whipped him:
"God is angry with the wicked . . ." and "Ye shall fear every man, his
mother and his father, saith the Lord . . ." (KJV)

A neighbor child died after a beating when Emilio was four and
that father was convicted of child abuse. From then on Emilio was
only "clipped" with the buckle—for such offenses as spilling his
milk—and by then Emilio's father had only to threaten with the belt
to get instant obedience. The thunderous quotations, however, so
impressed the boy that when he was asked to select some scriptures
to recite at a Christmas program, Emilio astonished everyone when
he chose to quote—

> "The fearful, and unbelieving, and the abominable and
> murderers and whoremongers and sorcerers and idola-
> ters and all liars shall have their part in the lake which
> burneth with fire and brimstone . . . Depart from me, ye
> cursed, into everlasting fire . . ." (KJV)

A Hell-Bound Boy

Emilio in jail seemed to be a small lost child in a cage, his big brown
eyes half-empty and pleading, until he stood up to shake hands with
us. With his Afro he was as tall as anyone in the room. His skin was
honey-colored, his trousers were carefully pressed, his hand trem-
bled, and his voice quavered as he greeted us.

Luiz said to me, "Emilio isn't kowtowing to you in the hope that
you can help him. He was raised to be submissive and polite. He
jumps to run errands for other inmates without being asked. He
obeyed the pornographer out of respect for someone older."

Emilio greeted me by saying, "It is so hot and stuffy we can
hardly breathe. It's hell." Luiz explained that Emilio's mother often
locked him in a closet at night for punishment and he would have
nightmares of being choked by the devil who would come with a
belt. "I never knew how many spoiled-garbage people there are,"
Emilio said, "until I was locked up here. I now know what the Bible
means about wailing and gnashing of teeth."

When four-year-old Emilio saw the ambulance come for his small
friend who had been beaten to death, and the police come to take
his father away, he had asked, "Why?" Emilio's father replied by
threatening him with the belt until he had memorized,

"If a man have a stubborn and rebellious son, which will not obey the voice of his father . . . or mother, and that when they have chastized him will not hearken unto them; then shall his father . . . lay hold on him . . . and all the men of the city shall stone him with stones that he die."

Little Emilio had again dared to ask, "But why?" And his father gave him the same answer over and over, "Spare the rod and spoil the child."

Emilio puzzled over what it meant to be a spoiled child, since his father said every day to his mother, "See now, you are spoiling that child." He decided that as food spoiled and was thrown into the garbage, so also some people became garbage and were carried away.

Emilio was eight when his mother left her husband and took him with her to live in the "barrio" with her mother. His father said scornfully, "Sure, take him away and spoil him good."

There were no more whippings, no more scripture verses, so Emilio worried that he was being spoiled, especially when he began to enjoy "wicked" things like TV and movies with stolen money. In middle school he became dependent upon a group of older boys who offered friendship and protection, taking him along when they went purse snatching. The spy game, following old people to see where they usually came and where they went, excited him; and running to snatch a purse and escape with it was more adventuresome than any other kind of athletics.

After his first arrest, Emilio was released to his mother "without punishment" because of his good reputation at school and because the police told the court that he was a young boy influenced by older ones who led him into trouble. Emilio, however, felt that the wrath of God had indeed descended upon him. His mother confined him to the apartment after school and weekends and threatened to send him back to his father. He tried to be good but he knew that he was spoiled, for his heart was in the street and in the movie houses. He fell behind in school, stunned by his arrest and the punishing exile from his friends, day-dreaming and listless.

The school psychologist said, "This youngster must go to the boys' club or get involved with some athletics." His mother refused at first, but finally registered Emilio for a soccer program in the park. His friends found him there and welcomed him like a hero home from a prisoner-of-war camp. They loaned him money and helped him slip out of the apartment to go to the movies after his mother was asleep.

One January night in 1972, eighty-year-old Mrs. Leen left her apartment to walk two blocks to the drug store, having forgotten to fill an essential prescription. She fought to keep her purse when Emilio playfully ran past her and grabbed for it, because she dared not lose the prescription. She slipped on the ice and broke her hip.

End of Emilio's First Criminal Career

Confronted with the evidence of her son's despicable act, Emilio's mother gave the police his father's telephone number, saying that she was no longer responsible for the boy. His father, an illegal immigrant with precarious employment, could not come until the weekend. Emilio waited at the detention center, terrified of what his father would do, hunched up alone, his thumb in his mouth, until other bored inmates—finding it amusing that Emilio was so easily intimidated and scared—began to play "cat and mouse" games to tease and to humiliate him. When asked how the other inmates punished him, Emilio could only stammer and quote scripture:

". . . abominable . . . whoremongers, sorcerers, idolaters, liars."

Luiz uses the word "sorcery" to explain the impact of punishment upon Emilio. The second arrest and incarceration was a searing punishment for the twelve-year-old—more so than for other inmates because Emilio's background of over-protection made him more innocent, naïve, docile, and emotionally defenseless.

"His father was the first sorcerer, with that whip," Luiz said. "And Emilio is still haunted by a morbid fascination with hell—and with prison as hell. He sees other inmates as sent by the devil. The juvenile court record says that Emilio was released without punishment in the case of Mrs. Leen, because he was a weak boy who needed his father's strong hand! Emilio considered himself harshly and bitterly punished: rejected by his mother, humiliatingly punished by other inmates, then exiled to New England and his father."

Emilio folded and unfolded his hands on the table as he told us about it: "I wish I could have told that old lady that I didn't mean to

. . . that I didn't want her to fall . . . that I was sorry . . . that I would like to do something to make it up to her."

The juvenile court's "mild lecture" was a cruel confirmation to him that he was spoiled, garbage, damned. The judge told Emilio that Mrs. Leen, who had been so happy in her own apartment, would now spend the rest of her life confined to a nursing home, which she hated.

"You see," Luiz said, "the court damned him with no chance for forgiveness, literally affirming the hell which Emilio suspected to be inevitable. This was a far harsher punishment than any of his father's beatings, or being half-drowned in the detention-center toilet by the kangaroo court."

Luiz showed me a letter from Emilio's pastor saying much the same: "If only he could have talked to Mrs. Leen, if Emilio could have been taken to the nursing home to apologize, perhaps he could then have heard the gospel. As it was he came to New England stone-deaf to anything we could say, condemning himself to a damnation which made his subsequent criminal career almost inevitable."

Emilio's stepmother did not want the boy. She had never seen him before and his guitar practice gave her headaches. Emilio's father was working overtime to pay for a second-hand car and had no time to take Emilio anywhere except to church. Father and son hardly ever had a sustained conversation.

Emilio often joined other thirteen-year-olds who would slip from the balcony of the church to talk on the front steps, where Emilio met some other rejects and some addicts and drug pushers who also came at times to sit there.

"No drugs for me," Emilio told us. "But I met those guys I could, you know, relate to . . ."

The officers of the congregation called the police to remove the pushers from the church steps; and finding drugs, the cops carted off everyone, including Emilio. He swore to his father that he had never used any drugs; but his father listened instead to a school official who thought he was coming to Emilio's defense, saying, "If these boys use a bit of pot, it is because they have a hard time, as Spanish-speaking kids in an English-language school."

That night Emilio's father threatened him over and over with the belt and thunderous scoldings—using every biblical word of judg-

ment he could remember. Then at 2:00 A.M. his father turned Emilio
out of the house, telling the thirteen-year-old never to return until
he was ready to be an obedient son.

Emilio walked dark streets, shivering, frightened, not knowing
where to go, until he encountered one of the drug pushers he had
met on the church steps. The pusher took him home, gave him a
"dose" to ease his psychological pain, listened to him talk, and let
him sleep it off. Two days later Emilio went to school, where a
counselor phoned to ask if he could return home. The boy went
back, docile and submissive, and all might have gone well if he had
not been in debt to the drug pusher, who offered to let Emilio work
off the debt.

"This was the moment," Luiz said, "when Emilio—the court
would say—deliberately chose to commit a criminal act. He was no
longer the sweet little schoolboy that the court could release to his
parents with a wrist-slap. Emilio, himself, had a horror of drugs,
often quoting his pastor, who had said that 'drugs are the devil's
grease to smooth the road to hell.' So where were the counselors,
the school psychologists, the people charged with helping troubled
youngsters when Emilio began to feel a need for drugs to ease his
pain and depression?"

"Where?" I asked.

"Giving superficial, irrelevant lectures to him *because no one
knew Emilio well enough to help him*. Oh, the police didn't have to
watch very long before they caught Emilio selling the 'devil's
grease.' But Emilio got his best advice from other prisoners in the
police tank the night he was arrested again. Older teenagers there
told him that he need not go to prison if he got a good attorney, one
costing $5,000. Emilio's father worked for less than four dollars an
hour, most of the family income went for food and rent. So what
was his next option?"

The other inmates told Emilio that he was sure to go to prison if
he had a court-appointed lawyer, since a newspaper had demanded
a crack-down on people who were selling drugs to kids. They also
warned Emilio that the detention home, where the kangaroo court
had tortured him, would seem like heaven compared to the state
reformatory where drug pushers went. So they advised him to run
away if he got out on bail. An inmate gave him the telephone
number of someone who would help and protect him, since

teenagers on the run make cooperative and pliable crime partners for older criminals to exploit. Silberman in *Criminal Violence/ Criminal Justice* reported how some criminal syndicates observe youngsters for recruitment as athletic scouts do. A *New York Times* editorial, May 1, 1977 said: ". . . the cream of inner-city youth . . . are recruited precisely because they are bright, resourceful, courageous and loyal." They have grown up in communities where juvenile employment is estimated to reach 65 per cent. The *Times* then tells of a fifteen-year-old, driving a $12,000 car, making $1,000 bets on schoolyard basketball games.

When Emilio was released to his stepmother on $50 bail he telephoned the number and was told to wait on a distant street corner where a car would pick him up. He was three states away from home, vulnerable and in debt to Rito, his criminal employer, before Emilio learned what was going to be required of him.

Horrified, he wept and prayed. Later he said to Luiz, "God turns a deaf ear to sinners in hell."

Emilio's Third Criminal Career

"Rito worked another sorcery on Emilio," Luiz said. "Sometimes he threatened the boy with a knife, warning Emilio that he was already wanted by the police for other murders. At other times he indulged Emilio with a lush life-style and a kind of camaraderie which the boy had never experienced. Emilio was also entranced with sexual experience before the camera. His respect for the purity of women, from his strict Pentecostal upbringing, forced Rito to find persuasive agruments: "Why are you in this hell of a mess? Because you are a Puerto Rican, a victim of American colonialism."

Emilio was not much persuaded by Rito's argument that "pornography to corrupt the imperialist-colonialist system was a good joke on the Yankee oppressors"; Rito was half-Colombian, half-Dominican; but he did introduce Emilio to some Puerto Rican revolutionaries—some young people who thrilled Emilio with a vision that their revolution was going to end drug pushing, vice, pornography, exploitation.

"For a moment the sorcerer's spell was broken," Luiz said. "The revolutionaries told Emilio that it was his duty to run away from the oppressive system that had entrapped him into crime, and they offered to hide him in Puerto Rico if he would join their cause. Up to that time, Emilio had thought of goodness as something passive— as simply refraining from evil, staying home to do nothing. Now he was elated to see a way out of hell."

"But Emilio didn't go to Puerto Rico."

"No, Rito got him off into another state without money and got his claws deeper into Emilio by promising him to help him save enough money to get to Puerto Rico. This was when I came into the picture," Luiz continued. "Whereas I tried to persuade him to turn himself in, Rito fired up Emilio's fears of police and prison and en- couraged his dream of escape to Puerto Rico as a better alternative. Also the pornographic pictures, in which Emilio's face was some- times visible, gave Rito a stronger whip-hand over the boy. Emilio had only to imagine those photos in the hands of his father and the police for fear to cast another sort of spell."

"But Emilio did telephone you collect every week."

"Yes, and I was soon able to tell him that New England author- ities knew nothing of his crimes in any other state, that his drug charges could be reduced to one count of selling marijuana, that I could promise him a suspended sentence so he could go back home and return to school if he turned himself in."

But Emilio said to Luiz on the phone, "Maybe the cops and the court don't know what I've been doing with Rito, but God knows."

Luiz said to me, "I guess Emilio saw himself through Rito's eyes as a weak character, living off vice, but not having Rito's courage to take his life into his own hands, as one who like Jonah had to try to run away from God's judgment."

"Jonah found there was no escape," I said.

"So did Emilio. He quoted scripture over long-distance phone calls, condemning himself for recruiting youngsters for pornog- raphy: "Whoso shall offend one of these little ones . . . it were better for him that a millstone were hanged around his neck and that he were drowned . . ."

Rito said to Emilio, "The cops will tell you any sort of lie to get you to turn yourself in, then they forget their promises." And he told many such stories of deception which he had heard in prison. He also quoted his own "scriptures" to Emilio:

"You have to stew in your own juice."

"When you've made your bed you have to lie in it."

So Emilio concluded, after much reflection about his inevitable punishment: "I've got it coming."

Luiz and I went to a retired juvenile court judge who sometimes gives counsel to attorneys who seek to give aid to children in court. "What should the courts do," we asked, "when Emilio is scared to help the police apprehend Rito? Rito warned that Emilio would be knifed, even in prison."

"Especially in prison," the judge replied. "It is easiest there. I find it ironic that our society punishes an alienated youngster by confirming his exile: first school suspension, then 'putting him on ice for a while,' then other kids telling him to 'get lost' when he comes out. So he does."

"A kind of damnation," I said.

Luiz nodded. "The hell Emilio fears is actually a freezing out of life. Although he speaks of the 'fires of hell' he also says, over and over, that life has somehow 'left him out in the cold.' Won't a boy like Emilio plunge deeper and deeper into crime—becoming another Rito—unless someone finds a way for him to quit punishing himself?"

"From what you tell me," the judge replied, "Emilio will certainly be victimized and criminalized in prison. Sir Walter Moberly says that we can be forgiven for hurting other people's bodies in punishment but never for hurting their souls. It may be all right for a judge to say, 'You deserve to be hanged' but not to say, 'You deserve to be damned' for that is evil."

"Emilio says it to himself," Luiz said. "Poisoned, I suppose, by a self-hate which knows no forgiveness. And how can he forgive himself until others forgive him first?"

"Who?" I asked.

"Not his father or mother who firmly believe in punishment and that, as Emilio says, he has it coming."

"Then is there no one?" I asked.

Later, after Emilio went to the reformatory, Luiz was the only one who ever went to see him or who wrote to him and sent gifts. "Isn't it ironic," he said, "that a boy who so needed a family should fall into the hands of an exploitative pornographer who was able and willing to play the role of affectionate father. Couldn't his church even yet find another family who would adopt him, at least write him letters?"

A clue to our puzzle, in a time when many are concerned about 'child abuse': Ruth Inglis, *Sins of Our Fathers* (New York: St. Martin's Press, 1978), warns that the psychological battering of minds and spirits may be more serious child abuse than battered bodies. Edgar Friedenberg, *The Vanishing Adolescent* (Boston: Beacon Press, 1959), describes the process whereby many youngsters are "sickened and terrified," their pride destroyed, and are convulsed with humiliation so that control may be "restored at a less than human level." Juvenile crime, as we see in several of these stories, is frequently a way in which a youngster tries to grow up and take control of his own life, to liberate himself when society fails him. Friedenberg describes the role of school counselors, and Paul Goodman, *Growing Up Absurd* (New York: Random House, 1956), shows how society itself oppresses the young.

EXPELLED PUPIL RETURNS TO ASSAULT TEACHER IN CLASS

A thirteen-year-old boy recently charged with assaulting a teacher has been arrested for manslaughter in the death of fourteen-year-old Joseph Z. in his schoolyard on Thursday. The arrest was announced simultaneously with the release of a school-board report showing that assaults on teachers by students have increased 77 per cent since 1971 and assaults on students 85 per cent.

In a press conference the Police Commissioner blamed the murder on the presence of so many juvenile drug addicts, robbers, and muggers released by the courts back into the schools, without punishment or therapy. He said that hundreds of incidents of teachers threatened with knives and guns, hit by chains and sticks, are not even counted in the assault statistics. The Commissioner left the press conference to meet with an Ad Hoc Committee of Parents and Teachers who are demanding that the thirteen-year-old, as a warning to other youths, be held in jail until he can be tried in an adult court. "The city can no longer tolerate such assaults in the schools," the Commissioner said.

Newspaper story about Bertie

CHAPTER 4

Bertie

"I paid my debt to society," Bertie said, explaining why he feels free for more crime. *"I paid and I'll pay again. Nothing's free."*

A FATHER STOOD OVER THE BODY of his dead child, vowing vengeance against thirteen-year-old Bertie, who, over and over, had been punished for bringing his knife to school.

"Why?" the father screamed with rage over the schoolyard stabbing.

Bertie had two weeks earlier been suspended for striking a teacher. The next day he had invaded her classroom to confront her again, so a committee in the neighborhood was organized to demand that Bertie be "well punished" for the murder—as a warning to other pupils who were bringing weapons to school and who were responsible for vandalism, rape, and assault on school property.

Two teachers began a quiet investigation to find out what had happened to this boy they had known to be well-behaved and wanting to learn, even though Bertie apparently was not as intelligent as the others. Was he a battered child, a victim of bad company, a child from a welfare family?

No, Bertie's mother had a good job at the post office and he had never been abused at home or neglected. His father was poorly educated, a petty thief who had been in and out of jail; but he and his wife were kind and loving with their son. Bertie had been spanked as a small child, but his parents had tried to be consistent and just in punishment. They had explained to Bertie that any misbehavior had a price which had to be paid, no matter how much a parent or child might want to make an exception. For the most part, Bertie was a quiet obedient boy who was "bad" only when he got anxious because his father had not showed up for a time, while hiding from the police

As to "bad company," the investigating teachers found to their surprise that Bertie had no association with any of the "bad crowd," the gang that controlled the streets. Bertie had learned who the troublemakers were so that he could studiously avoid them.

A Knife for Protection

The two teachers disagreed on the influence of the neighborhood. Miss V., a graduate of Columbia University Teacher's College, had taught in the area for ten years, and had chosen to live there so that she could be active in neighborhood political and social groups, even shaming other teachers with her devotion and her demands for evaluation and innovation. She said that Bertie's mother couldn't find a better place to live than her insurance-company-financed apartment.

Mr. W., in his mid-fifties, was burned-out by years of discouragement in inner-city schools and was retiring to go into business. He said, "I agree with the clergyman who said the architects of those mass-custody apartments should be given a "Dachau Award" for creating a concentration camp which successfully dehumanizes children. It is hard to get the truth about anything there. People will tell the cops one story, the teachers another, the social workers a third, and the reporters a fourth version of the same incident. And they'll all tell another story the next day."

The two teachers agreed that any urban development that "crawls with children" has similar problems, including predators; many women carry mace and a whistle in their purses for the same reasons that many youngsters take weapons to school.

Miss V. explained: "Bertie's mother told us that he began hiding under the bed, refusing to go to school, when he was about eight. So his father got Bertie a knife and showed the boy how to use it to protect himself from older children who extorted money. About every other year a new gang emerges, beginning with eleven- or twelve-year-olds who start taking money and lunches from younger children, then turn to extortion, asking modest amounts for protection. Bertie had to pay ten cents twice a week for safe passage to school. When he told the other children that he had no allowance or money, he was ordered to steal it from his mother's purse."

"She actually gave him the twenty cents a week," Mr. W. said. As Bertie got older, the rate went up: twenty-five cents, fifty cents, finally a dollar a week when he entered junior-high school."

"Did school authorities know about this?" I asked.

"Yes, the police arrest the ring leaders from time to time but it is such a profitable racket that arrests don't really stop anything. Where else can kids get hundreds of dollars a week? There is always a new group ready to take over when the former ring leaders go to reform school. Like hustling, selling numbers, or pot, this kind of petty racket is almost impossible for police to handle if large numbers of youngsters get involved. It is often the school monitors, while helping the smaller children cross the streets, who collect the "ten-cent tips." Once a boy shows a knife or gun he then doesn't usually pay anymore. In fact, a boy with a gun is likely to be invited to share in the take, keeping half of all he collects.

"Did Bertie's mother know he was taking the knife to school?"

"Of course," Miss V. replied. "She didn't know quite what to say when he was punished for it, because she knew he needed it to get to school unharmed."

Typically, she punished him privately and defended him publicly, as when he "borrowed" another child's tricycle. She told the neighbor that some other child had lent it to him, that it wasn't Bertie who stole it; then punished him severely in private, explaining that, "You can't have anything without paying for it and it costs more to steal than to work."

The two teachers reported other incidents in which Bertie learned a sort of cost-accounting approach to crime and punishment, in which once you have paid for what you did you are forgiven. Bertie's father told him that he was hiding from the police, because he was not quite ready yet to pay his debt to society. His father said, "A man who steals is a kind of slave until he pays his debt, then he's free again."

"One hears the same cost-accounting interpretation of punishment on the school ground," Mr. W. said. "The coaches understand it on the athletic field. They fight to pay a debt, then they can be friends again. And there is a great deal of calculating to determine whether certain types of misbehavior are worth the cost. One may refrain from certain acts to avoid costly punishment, but not if it is a matter of honor or necessity. You have to understand that Bertie had to carry that knife to school, no matter what the cost, as a matter of masculine honor. Even capital punishment is no deterrent in cases of honor, passion, or necessity."

Miss V. added, "Bertie felt great shame and guilt because he did not mean to kill his assailant; but now that he has been punished, now that his debt is paid, he is technically free from onus. Some lower-class people here can't understand why a previous felony conviction prevents them from getting certain jobs. For example, a convicted molester of little girls protested discrimination when he was denied a job as playground supervisor, saying, 'But I've paid my debt.'"

"Did Bertie calculate the cost when he stabbed the boy?"

Mr. W. nodded. "Afterwards he assumed that he would go to the electric chair. He was quite astonished to discover that he was too young."

"But punishment does prevent some crime if the price is high?"

"Not really," Mr. W. said. "If one person is unwilling to pay a high price, someone else, especially a kid, is more adventurous or desperate."

"When Bertie was seven or eight," Miss V. added, "he readily paid dimes to his extortioners because he didn't want his head hit against the pavement again. Nor was his mother willing to have him pay such a price. Another mother, who cooperated with the police in the arrest of some of the extortioners, was rewarded with an eight-year-old in the hospital with a split skull."

Mr. W. was cynical. "Even our principal has accused parents of child abuse when he should have known that the child was beaten by extortioners. One mother actually admitted to child abuse rather than risk punishment from the youngsters who had actually hurt her child."

His School Punishment

"Bertie was first warned and scolded for bringing the knife to school, then he was spanked. You must understand," Mr. W. said, "that corporal punishment by us is strictly forbidden by law, but the school board has a confidential, unpublicized policy that drastic action can be taken for possession of knives, guns, and for assaults on teachers."

"Teachers in the primary grades hit the youngsters all the time," Miss V. said. "Bertie told us of twelve incidents when he was slapped in class, once by a new, idealistic teacher who told me she would never under any circumstances hit a child. She tried calling on parents to enlist their help and cooperation but never found any of them at home. She tried positive reenforcement, giving candy and gifts for good behavior, but even in the third grade she had many kids who were disruptive, sneaky, hyperactive, and too many of them in need of adequate personal attention."

"Bertie was her pet," Mr. W. said. "His mother was home and actively cooperated with the teachers. Bertie was hurt when that teacher despaired and quit, because she was so scared of knives that she was unwilling to turn her back long enough to write on the board. There should be two teachers in every class here as long as we have so many disruptive, troubled, and failing children; but when one teacher quits like that, the youngsters often have an untrained substitute for the rest of the year."

"I'm sure she gave Bertie his confiscated knife back when she left," Miss V. said. "She knew he wanted to be law-abiding, but that he was naked and vulnerable without that knife."

"The knife he killed with," I said.

"Yes he was doomed either way, wasn't he," Miss V. replied. "He couldn't survive without it or with it. It is ironic that, because he was his teacher's pet, Bertie once escaped punishment—tipped off that the police were coming. Others who were caught made sure that Bertie was punished for something else a few days later. No amount of punishment will disarm our kids until the war is over—between pupils, between pupils and teachers."

"Everyone is armed for war except the teachers," Mr. W. said. "Seventy thousand of us get assaulted each year in this country and most of us here are scared and the kids are scared, too, that they may be losing life's battle even before it begins."

"You're overstating that," Miss V. said. "Most of our pupils still hope for a miracle. They carry their knives to fight to hold out until the miracle occurs."

"I'm quitting," Mr. W. said. "I see the calm of a soldier who is
meeting machine-gun fire from the enemy when I look into the eyes
of some of my best pupils, who see punishment as my weapon in
the pupil-teacher war. The effects of the battle may be devastating
but the courageous, honorable kid, with fight in his soul, does not
surrender. He would rather die."

"You are exaggerating again," Miss V. said.

"Oh?" Mr. W. raised his eyebrows. "Then why are so many kids
like Bertie already dead to learning, to school, often to hope? From
age six they are continually knocked around, first by other pupils,
then by the teachers who get numb when the students become
sullen and disruptive. First the youngsters finger the knives in their
pockets for reassurance, then—wanting to belong—a boy like
Bertie becomes vulnerable to the subculture of adolescence. What
other kids say about punishment is what matters most. The murder
and Bertie's downfall were pretty much the result of pupil interpretation of his suspension."

One day Bertie was accused of throwing a rock at a teacher's car.
He was not the one who did it, and he said so, but the principal and
the teacher did not believe him, because several jealous youngsters
said that they saw him do it.

"If there had been a hearing," Mr. W. said, "Bertie could have
produced witnesses, but youngsters are not allowed a fair trial
before being punished at school. Our weak principal preferred to
let Bertie off lightly, with the warning that, if 'any such thing ever
happened again, Bertie would lose his coveted place in the experimental social-studies program.' I think the principal was frankly
scared of the boys who really threw the rocks."

The federally-funded social-studies project selected boys to
spend time with a city official, learning about the job. Bertie was
assigned to an electrical inspector and was so interested that his
schoolwork was blossoming. Two days after the rock-throwing incident Bertie had a fight with the substitute teacher who, after six
months, was not teaching anything in the math class; she was
simply trying to keep order. "I would have rebelled myself," Mr. W.
said.

Bertie went to the pencil sharpener without permission and the
substitute teacher knocked him into a window and it broke. She
then lied to the principal, making the incident more serious than it
actually was, perhaps because she thought Bertie really was the

boy who had thrown rocks at her car. Bertie did raise a hand in self-defense, but again a fair hearing would have cleared Bertie of responsibility for breaking the window. The principal did not check with the other pupils who witnessed the incident when Bertie was marched to the office for a confrontation with three adults, none of whom would listen to him. His three-day suspension from school meant being withdrawn from the electrical-inspector project which meant so much to him.

"He was crushed," Mr. W. said. "That project was probably Bertie's last chance to succeed in school and maybe it was his last chance for a non-criminal career."

During the next several days a number of teachers rallied to Bertie's defense as they learned the truth from other pupils. School officials, however, made public statements defending themselves and the substitute teacher said that Bertie was guilty of various provocative acts in class. At the same time the principal privately told his teachers that the school system had acted criminally, sending one inexperienced teacher into an eighth-grade math class which she was not qualified to teach, and expecting her to police such an unruly group. Then he went to a parents' meeting where he said the pupils "lie all the time," slander the teachers, and that the substitute was justified in punishing Bertie as she did when she could stand his disruption no longer.

The neighborhood was tense and other boys in the class chided Bertie for not fighting back like a man, and began questioning his manhood. "If he did not hit back some way," Miss V. explained, "he was a 'fairy,' a pariah who could not look other males square in the face."

"But note the interesting twist here," Mr. W. said. "Normally a boy here would never hit back if a woman teacher strikes him, because teachers, as mother figures, can slap their wrists, twist their ears, and punish them in ways they will not take from a male teacher. Men at our school are generally intuitive enough to avoid hitting boys, but, even so, they often lash back at male teachers with their fists when tongue lashings or other punishments seem unfair or too humiliating."

The consensus on the street was that Bertie's substitute teacher should not be allowed "to get away with it." Boys in her class discussed fire bombing her house or car, but cooler heads prevailed. She was a young, inexperienced woman, so the proper and manly thing for Bertie was to go back to class to offer and demand apologies. Bertie was to swallow his pride enough to say he was sorry if he had done anything and was to offer to shake hands in a truce if she would help him get back into the electrical-inspector position. So the next morning he marched into class and asked to be heard.

The teacher was furious at the interruption; she was scared and demanded that Bertie leave—which he refused to do without a chance to speak. She knew that she had lied and now the whole class was cheering Bertie on, saying that he had a right to be heard. Foolishly she fled to the principal's office, hysterically shrieking that Bertie had returned to hit her again. She then ran to the custodian, saying that she could no longer bear being insulted and abused. She fled in her car to tell the story to the newspaper and never again returned to the school.

"I can almost laugh now," Miss V. said. "But there was panic in the halls, with pupils from her class running wild. The police were called and Bertie was almost arrested. The newspaper headline read: EXPELLED PUPIL RETURNS TO ASSAULT TEACHER IN CLASSROOM. This time the principal believed the witnesses. The next day the police were sent to track down Bertie to apologize."

The police couldn't find Bertie because the other pupils, assuming that he would be arrested were hiding him. Bertie hid for two days, then returned to school after learning that he was cleared and forgiven. But before he even got inside, he was confronted by an angry acquaintance who charged him with a knife. Bertie, trembling with anger over the unfairness of his treatment, slashed back and killed him.

"Why did the other boy threaten him?" I asked.

"No one knows for sure," Mr. W. replied. "Gossip says that Bertie was reputed to have made a remark about a girl. It was again a matter of honor. Joe demanded an apology and Bertie refused to apologize for something he never said."

Court Punishment

Bertie was very repentant in court, emotionally accepting the necessity of "paying for what he had done." He was terribly punished by his own conscience, having nightmares about the blood on the knife, the arrest, being handcuffed, and jailed. No one at the court can now adequately explain why Bertie was kept in jail for months.

The judge said, "It was a mistake, even though we have a tremendous backlog of work and get months behind because we are short of staff."

A social worker said, "It happened because he was charged with murder and there was the confusion under the new law over his transfer from juvenile to adult court. Also he had an inept lawyer."

The attorney said, "Bertie was kept in jail because his mother, different from most black people, trusted the justice system and kept believing what people told her."

"She also believed he was in jail to 'pay his debt,' which justice required," Mr. W. explained, "and the judge confirmed this in her eyes when, after pre-sentencing negotiations, he sentenced Bertie to the amount of time he had actually spent in jail, plus a short suspended sentence to put him under the supervision of a juvenile probation officer."

"Everyone agreed that the important thing was to get Bertie out of jail and into the fine program in auto mechanics which interested him," Miss V. said.

Mr. W. disagreed. "Everyone? Not Bertie. He got what he wanted, but seethed inside at having to sit silently all the time while other people discussed what to do with him, never letting him say anything but 'yes' or 'no' at the prodding of his lawyer."

Bertie saw that gag as part of his punishment, and his feeling that his "debt was paid" was strongly confirmed by the hero's welcome he received back on his own street. He saw new respect in the eyes of the gang members he had formerly feared, for now he was a "killer" and one who had come home after a few months of punishment, free to begin a successful criminal career. His reputation made it possible for him to be offered a splendid job—stealing car parts for the operator of a junk yard—which he could begin even before completing his auto repair course. By the time he was seventeen, Bertie had his own Cadillac.

When I met Bertie, he was not at all as I had expected. He was tall, heavy, awkward—having grown nearly two feet since the murder. He no longer seemed shy or afraid, yet he was inarticulate, with a moody sort of silence with friends as well as strangers.

"Do you ever go to church, Bertie?" I asked.

"Sometimes."

"With a girl?"

"No, I jive the music."

"The syncopation?"

"I like the selection, 'Jesus Paid It All' and 'Nothing But the Blood of Jesus'. Some time, maybe, I'll answer the altar call."

Bertie's pastor is elderly and not well. He confesses to ignorance about Bertie, never really having known the boy until after he came out of jail. The pastor said, "Bertie's making lots of money, I hear. Old folks like me he doesn't talk to; and young folks like him, he wants them to think he's a big man already with women and cars . . . so he stands apart. He tells them nothing much, not even his girls."

"His former teachers say he swaggers now," I said. "That he feels free to break the law because he's paid his debt to society before, and can do it again."

The old pastor raised his hands. "But what's inside that boy? At Christmas he sent a big basket of fruit to the family whose boy he killed, a peace offering. You say he comes to church for the music? I say he hardly hears it because he has no peace. He has heard that the boy he killed just wanted to scratch him with the knife, to draw some blood to pay for an insult. So Bertie hurts inside."

The family of the boy he killed threw Bertie's Christmas basket of fruit into the middle of the street.

A clue: William Shannon in *The New York Times* (September 8, 1976) expressed the concern of many parents who feel that when they take their children to school, they are "delivering them into enemy territory," where they experience what Nat Hentoff has called "the evil flowering of crime, vandalism, and the breakdown of authority." Gerald Mendel, psychiatrist, warns in *Pour Décoloniser L'Enfant* (Paris: Payot, 1971) that the breakdown of traditional authorities will in the future require *more cooperation with children as equals* with adults, more listening to children by adults, with adults learning from children as well as the other way around. Howard James says, "It is terrible what we do to children," because teachers and social workers lack the training, authority, and resources to do their jobs in today's society. Rollo May in *Power and Innocence* (New York: Norton, 1972) warns that "the state of powerlessness, which leads to apathy, is the source of violence."

WHAT DO YOU MEAN?
Children's Rights!

Our major local industry has been damaged by a ring of blackmailers who have preyed on tourists, offering them "sex shows" by young teenagers. A local clergy group has petitioned for the release of the chief witness and offender, a fourteen-year-old who refuses to identify the adult vulture who may now be trying to recruit your child.

These clergy say that the boy has "rights" because he is "gay" and needs protection from the police (and not from his adult criminal partner), because he is a minor.

A fourteen-year-old murderer is now tried as an adult. So if this boy has willingly blackmailed, has perhaps been a prostitute, is he any longer a child to be coddled?

His refusal to identify his exploiter is proof of his complicity. Such slime should be locked up on bread and water until he puts his finger on this vicious adult that only he can identify. Refusing to do that, he has no rights at all, other than those accorded to any adult criminal.

In our book, *gay* means "depraved" and so he should, in any case, be locked up for his own protection and for the protection of other youngsters he may yet corrupt.

Editorial from EX-COP, a weekly
police report in Hector's town

CHAPTER 5

Hector

"I don't care how they punish me," Hector said. *"It can't be worse than my dad bashing me with an iron skillet. Pretty soon you get numb and don't care anymore."*

"I GOT INVOLVED WITH HECTOR, this fourteen-year-old who was arrested for blackmailing foreign tourists," said Michael S., a young Methodist clergyman, "when I learned that this boy had been in our Sunday School. As I talked to Hector's teachers and to others who had worked with him, I saw that our church bears a lot of blame for his falling into a criminal career. I'm also trying to help Hector because the justice establishment is abusing the boy."

Hector looked more like the president of the church youth group than a blackmailer who had been earning hundreds of dollars a week. But officials of the resort city—the mayor, the police, the D.A.'s office, and the Chamber of Commerce—were so angry that they were ready to pillory him, because Hector refused to identify the adult criminal who had enlisted him in the blackmail scheme. Newspapers were calling Hector's partner "the most vicious criminal ever to invade our city" and "a menace to our key industry."

"The police," the pastor said, "seem to forget that Hector was only thirteen and also a victim. Yet he has been brutally treated, even by the court psychiatrist, in an effort to force information from him that Hector loyally refuses to give."

"Why does he refuse?" I asked.

Pastor Michael looked sad. "Hector feels that the blackmailer is

59

the only true, dependable, loving friend he has ever had; so the boy will die rather than betray him. Why, I must ask, did our congregation fail to provide him with a true, affectionate, dependable friend during the years he was around our church?"

"What about Hector's family?"

"His sister has disappeared and his father is too embarrassed to be of much help. In February or early March of 1974 a widow on welfare reported to her social worker, somewhat reluctantly, that her young daughter was in the hands of a pimp who was using youngsters in a blackmail scheme. The pimp would approach a tourist walking alone at night in quest of adventure and would offer a new experience: a girl-boy sex show and perhaps more. The youngsters were trained to steal the tourist's credit cards or driver's license and when the tourist learned that the girl was only thirteen, he usually paid generously to get his papers back."

"How did Hector get into such a racket?"

"Theoretically, Hector and his sister were cared for by an aged, almost senile aunt—an alcoholic who was drunk much of the time—while their father, an interstate truck driver, was out of town. From the age of five or six, Hector was actually fed, washed, and cared for much of the time by a sister two years older, who was his co-conspirator in hiding the truth about a bad family situation from social workers and school officials. Their father and aunt always made a good impression on visitors. At one time the father tried to find a job that would keep him home evenings with his motherless children, and at another time he almost confessed his embarrassing secret to a social worker who had told him he didn't need her assistance because he had a large enough income to employ any help he needed.

"He nearly wept when he said, 'Damn it, they give you a manual with the truck, but a kid comes with no instructions whatever . . . on what to do if there's something wrong'."

Hector was a handsome youngster, small for his age, but skilled at athletics, a self-taught acrobat whose physical grace and agility made him delight his audiences. He was pleasant and clever at avoiding scoldings and criticism. His honest father was horrified to learn that seven-year-old Hector was stealing hubcaps along with a gang of older boys. He whipped Hector and threatened him with even worse whippings if it ever happened again. So by the time

Hector was ten he had been beaten almost to the point of numbness.

"Hector's father was not a religious man," Michael said, "but he believed that if a child had a taint, it could be whipped out of him; that the dose of punishment should be increased until there was a cure, especially an embarrassing taint like homosexuality. His father would have killed an older boy for sexual approaches to his son. What was he to do when he learned that eight-year-old Hector was the one making sexual overtures? His solution, as sometimes said in nineteenth-century England was 'if whipping doesn't stop it, then flog; if flogging doesn't stop it, then pillory; if that doesn't stop it, then hang.' And by the time Hector was thirteen, and arrested, his father was ready to hang him."

Hector, from an early age aware of a strong attraction to other males, tried hard to win their approval while in grade school by joining in their thefts and by intensive practice at acrobatics which won him admiring respect from other boys. He also had a sense of humor which could demolish an opposing baseball team. Hector had sympathy from other youngsters for being beaten so much at home, and for the most part they rejected the gossip that he was "queer," since he could hold other baseball teams nearly scoreless when he pitched. "He was," the pastor said, "essentially a moral, prudent kid who didn't try it again when his sexual overtures were rebuffed during the pre-pubescent, hanky-panky years. But when he was thirteen and he refused a girl offered to him so he could "prove his masculinity," he began to be teased at school.

"Even then," the pastor continued, "most of his close friends remained loyal to him, at least privately, and some of them set out to find gay friends for him. They found youngsters who 'hustled' on a highway bridge in a nearby community, youngsters who were involved in crime. They horrified Hector, who, nevertheless, welcomed their counsel and advice—since he had no other adequate source of information about his homosexuality."

With no encouragement from their father, Hector's sister had started taking the boy to the Methodist Sunday School when he was four. "The two children attended faithfully for years, with no adult seeming to care, until," Michael paused, puzzled how to explain it, "until there came a time, like old-time friendships between black and white boys in the south, when the gay boy was no longer ac-

ceptable as a friend and member of the church group. Once Hector
began to admit that he was gay and wanted to talk about it and ask
questions about it, the youngsters of the church youth group simply
dropped Hector and his sister."

School Punishment

Being athletic and strong, Hector responded to the teasing at
school by fighting a lot, even tackling groups of larger boys, and, as
a consequence, was quite often suspended.

"Did school officials not know that Hector was being molested
and teased for being gay, that he was, in fact, fighting in self-
defense?"

"No," Michael replied. "The teachers and the principal tell me
that they had no reason to think that athletic, well-adjusted Hector
was gay. In their eyes, gay kids were supposed to be sissies who
wore glasses, shrinking violets with limp wrists who want to wear
girl's clothing. And when the principal was confronted with
evidence that older, larger boys were molesting Hector—actually
teasing him with overt sexual propositions—he reluctantly assumed
it must be Hector's fault and called in his father, who was so angry
he almost hit the principal."

Only Hector was punished since he seemed to start the fights,
always responding to verbal taunts with his fists. The principal tried
to channel the fights into a boxing ring, where Hector was more
than able to hold his own, and threatened long-term suspension if
Hector continued to fight outside the ring. When next suspended,
and while he was hitch-hiking to go look for the gay boys on the
bridge, Hector met the adult blackmailer who was looking for a gay
boy who "wanted to make a lot of money fast."

"I had never before realized," Michael said, "the high price that
gay youngsters often pay for the fact that their families, friends,
and society reject them, for the fact that no one seems to care
about what happens to them. A gay boy like Hector is very vulnerable and a safe criminal partner—especially since he has nowhere
else to go but home where he fears a father who will beat him with
an iron skillet again."

"I really think," Michael said, "that the powers-that-be in this
town, after this blackmail thing was in newspapers, deliberately
passed the word to the cops and the court that, as a gay boy, Hector

was expendable. The D.A. actually told me that I could promise Hector release without punishment if he identified his partner, but that otherwise I was to tell Hector that his punishment was going to escalate to hell. So what Hector says about the court psychiatrist may be true! 'That psychiatrist is a fink who can't get a job any-where else.'"

"Hector insists that he will commit suicide rather than fall into the hands of that psychiatrist again. The psychiatrist swears to me, almost hysterically, that he only used hypnotism and threats of electric shock in an attempt to cure Hector's homosexuality, but I have seen a memo authorizing him to 'use all possible methods' to obtain from Hector the name of the adult blackmailer. Whatever he did, he scared Hector terribly."

Court Punishment

The Methodist judge, president of a Christian Businessmen's Breakfast Group, was angry at Michael's suggestion that Hector was being punished for his homosexuality. "The boy is a black-mailer who has helped bring great shame to this town, endangering its reputation for curious tourists."

"Can you say that a fourteen-year-old is definitely homosexual?"

"What does that mean? His chemistry is somehow mixed up. Every man who has interrogated Hector has found him getting seductive. To be frank, that's one reason they have been rough on the boy at times. I don't know how the typical cop reacts when a female whore gets seductive at arrest or interrogation, but I can tell you that many cops lose their cool and see red when a male whore does the same."

"Isn't whore a rather strong term for a youngster who insists that he was never sexually involved with any of the blackmailed people?"

The judge was red in the face. "We have no proof of that; or, as he says, that his relationship with the blackmailer was just paternal."

"Then isn't Hector entitled to be considered innocent until proven guilty?"

"We have conclusive proof of his blackmailing."

"But you called him a whore," I said, "which implies the sexual activity which he denies."

"Hector and that girl were offered as whores, so whether or not they honored that contract is beside the point. He's charged with blackmail, not a sexual offense."

"Won't the girl identify the blackmailer?"

"She was also loyal and has disappeared, perhaps to the blackmailer, which is the reason why we must keep Hector locked up. If he gets a chance he would run away to that man he has a crush on. He admits it."

"Hector's pastor says the boy's rights are being violated."

The judge got angry whenever the pastor was mentioned. "Hector can't go back to some innocent stage. The problem is deep in his personality and character. Maybe he didn't consciously realize he was trying to seduce me but he made me very uncomfortable. He has no family now, for all practical purposes, so I asked him where he could go if released by the court. He brazenly said he could find a man to live with."

"Shouldn't he be in a foster home?"

"Who would take him? Wouldn't he just run away to look for that blackmailer he's so crazy about? The pastor thinks some church people could take Hector into a home, but I know that most church members are embarrassed too. They don't want him in the church youth group."

"So he has to stay in jail?"

"Hector is a menace. The only way he knows to earn a living is through blackmail. What legal thing can he do, at his age, if he runs away again? He is a menace to homosexuals. If some gay man takes the boy in, out of sympathy for a poor runaway kid, that man could be arrested for kidnapping and for contributing to the delinquency of a minor—even if there is no sexual involvement. Don't you see how a boy like Hector can destroy gay men who want to be law-abiding? This boy refuses to admit that he has done anything wrong. If he was sorry and would show this by cooperating with the court, there might be some hope that he would not return immediately to criminal activity."

Hector never denied his blackmailing activity and described it as a kind of game. "We never did anything very wrong," he said. "We conned some guys who were out on the prowl at night, looking for something illegal. Some were fags who wouldn't admit it. Others, away from home, were looking for some sort of peep show or something. We just started to undress, fooled around a little, and gave them some laughs. If a guy tried to get one of us in bed we'd get hold of his driver's license—and he'd pay to get it back, not because he'd done anything much, but because he had a guilty conscience."

"Then you never had sex?"

"Not with any of those guys we shook down. Rumby (Hector's adult partner) called it 'teasing and taking.' All he ever offered was 'an unusual experience with two kids'—and he said that the experience we gave those guys was like the scare house at Disneyland. No sex, just a bad scare for kicks. And we taught them a lesson, too."

Perhaps one reason the police and other interrogators have so much trouble with Hector's story is that he is so moralistic.

"I'm not going to bed with anyone I don't love," he insisted. "If I had had sex with some of those guys I'd admit it, like I admit the blackmail. I think it served them right, don't you?" And about Rumby he added, "Rumby would never want to hurt anyone. In the reformatory he even nursed sick cockroaches."

Hector's Church

"Hector and his sister are remembered at our church," Michael said, "as polite youngsters whose clothes were clean but always lacked buttons. The last pastor once called in the home and left with the confident feeling that the children were well cared for, even though the father and aunt had no interest in church. No one knew that Sunday after Sunday the two kids went home to a dinner of peanut butter and potato chips. Hector speaks poignantly of his joy when his Sunday School teacher would bring a cake for someone's birthday and recalls that, at age nine, he used to wish that some church family would take him home to eat Sunday dinner with them."

"You said that the church should have provided Hector with the counseling and friends that he needed."

Michael nodded. "Even if other youngsters rejected Hector, we should have provided him with supportive adult friends. Only one of Hector's Sunday School teachers was ever aware of his problems. She told the pastor that someone should give special attention to the ten-year-old. She worked at a drug store and Hector sometimes walked a mile to see her there, even after he got involved with the blackmailer. He said of her, 'She was always friendly but was really too busy to talk to me. I mean she really had customers standing in line.'"

Now, too late, she had petitioned the court to ask for permission to take Hector into her home for some time. She would have gone to see him as soon as he was arrested, had she only known. As a juvenile, his name never appeared in the newspapers.

She said, "We talk a lot about saving the lost, but Hector was never really lost, was he? The church always had his name, address, and telephone number. Our church is so large that we can't be expected to remember all the children from non-church families who come here at one time or another."

Michael said, "Hector is numb from being beaten so much by his father, and from all the brutality of those who have interrogated him; but even more perhaps because of punishment to exile. He was suspended from school, was made unwelcome at the church youth group, was dropped by his neighborhood gang, and was then isolated in jail. The blackmailer and that hustling gang, you can be sure, gave him the affectionate personal attention he so desperately needed. Although we tried to find him a foster home or a group home for gay youngsters, the court insisted that Hector had to go to the reformatory until he was twenty-one."

Only later did I learn that Hector never was sentenced because he, too, disappeared. A compassionate court official and an anonymous church official helped him get away to another state where the boy was adopted by a young dentist, a Harvard graduate, who has paid for Hector's education at an excellent private school. As a result Hector was launched at a very young age into a profitable adult career and is now almost completely supporting himself and financing his own education. As a ski instructor and master ski stunt performer—largely in Europe—he has combined his acrobatics and ski interest into what Michael calls ". . . a marvelous performance. I'd love to see him, his sponsor says he is really dazzling the crowds."*

As social workers sometimes say, Hector "found his own place-

---

*Hector's actual sport, of course, is changed for his protection.

ment" with a man he met when he went skiing with his blackmailer-accomplice.

"I suppose the young dentist is gay?" I asked.

Michael opened his hands on the table. "Why should I ask? Hector is an adult now, acting responsibly, happy to be succeeding at school, loving and needing the applause. He found someone who cares; he has the affection he never got at home, school, or church. He is finding a meaningful, fulfilling place for himself in society. Do you mean he would have been better off in the reformatory until he is twenty-one?"

"Why do you suppose someone helped him run away?" I asked.

The pastor opened his Bible to read from the story of David and Jonathan: ". . . for the Lord sees not as a man sees; man looks on the outward appearance, but the Lord looks on the heart." He paused a moment, thoughtfully, then added: "The court was going to punish Hector for loyal friendship and other qualities of heart. I don't believe in punishing a youngster for something in his nature he cannot change. I agree with St. Paul, who says: "Let us no more pass judgment on one another, but rather decide never to put a stumbling block or hindrance in the way of a brother. I know and I am persuaded in the Lord Jesus that nothing is unclean in itself; but it is unclean for anyone who thinks it unclean" (Romans 14:13-14).

A clue: *Time* magazine, June 4, 1972, reported on juveniles who turn to adult criminals for affection and meaningful relationships otherwise denied to them. Speaking of juvenile prostitutes as "lost children" searching for families and for meaningful adult relationships, *Time* said, "They wander around lost and angry and it is hard to heal them. The public shelters are like jails. Street life is hard." And the Rev. Paul Shanley, priest assigned to work with runaway youngsters in Boston, reported in the *New York Times,* April 25, 1979, that many teen-age runaways are kicked out at home because they are gay. The Rev. Randolph Gibson, who operates a counseling center in Boston for teen-age homosexuals is quoted by the Associated Press as saying, "These youngsters die a strange internal death because as one tearfully put it: 'It's hell.'"

CHOIR SINGER ARRESTED AS THIEF AND GANG LEADER

A dozen boys and girls, aged twelve to fifteen, were arrested yesterday as they came to the garage of an abandoned house on Sixth Street, which was full of school typewriters, musical instruments, and athletic equipment stolen from area schools. The robberies were reputedly planned and directed by a fifteen-year-old girl, a student at one of the most often burglarized high schools, who has been well known as soloist for a popular youth choir.

Informers have told the police that the juvenile gang worked in concert with out-of-town fences, stealing whatever the adult criminals requested for delivery to out-of-state trucks which came to the garage every other week. The youngsters used a crowbar to break the metal chains which the school board authorized to replace weekend security patrols. Police regularly check doors and windows, hoping to catch young burglars in the act, but a member of the school board said, "The cops are no match for kids so numerous that they keep the cops under surveillance."

Newspaper report about Lena
from THE CORNERS SHOPPER

CHAPTER 6

Lena

"I'm just a scapegoat," Lena said. *"Nearly every kid in this project has done worse things than me; so why did they punish me and not them?"*

"WHY THE HOSTILITY?" The question was asked by two members of the usher board of the Fifth Street Missionary Baptist Church who were trying to help fifteen-year-old Lena Brown, arrested for masterminding a major theft ring.

Lena's arrest had shocked everyone in the church where she sang in the choir, because she was one of the best-liked, most able, most respected, and influential youngsters in her neighborhood. Sister Fanny and Mother Josephine, the two ushers, were also shocked by a seething anger they had never seen in Lena before. They expected the girl to be humble after her arrest, hurt if innocent, or embarrassed, or at least poised, cool, and self-confident as usual. Instead, Lena's anger was explosive as she said over and over, "Why me? Why me?"

Her school friends who were not involved in the thefts also reacted with an unusually angry hostility, "Why Lena?"

The two church ushers turned to Miss Eleanor, a Vista worker who knew Lena and her gang of friends very well, for an explanation of this unexpected behavior. "Is Lena angry because she didn't do it?"

"No," Miss Eleanor replied. "She's guilty."

"Then she's angry 'cause she got caught?" Sister Fanny hated to say that because she had great affection for Lena. "Or did she think she's different or better than other folks, and that therefore she shouldn't get caught?"

"To understand why Lena is hostile," the Vista worker replied, "requires you to see life as young people do here in The Corners and not as you saw it in Georgia when you were their age."

A sociologist described The Corners as one of the most promising urban neighborhoods in the north, with Italians and Jews increasingly replaced by Cubans, Dominicans, and Blacks from rural Georgia to provide a tri-ethnic balance. Urban redevelopment had cleared slums, built playgrounds, parks, and handsome new schools. Vista workers were creating healthy block organizations to facilitate political and social renewal. A major industry had recently moved South with the result of much unemployment especially among young people just out of high school. Street crime, according to Miss Eleanor, had increased to meet a need for spending money and as a protest against "the system" that failed to provide summer jobs for young people.

When she first came to the area in the fall of 1974, Miss Eleanor became interested in the plight of a Vietnam War veteran who had used his savings to open a badly-needed variety store, wanting to help Black people get a fair deal: quality merchandise at fair prices. He also wanted to provide jobs for Blacks and "set an example to unemployed kids to encourage others to go into business." He was therefore puzzled when his shop became a prime target for theft by the very young people he came to befriend and help. Miss Eleanor soon saw that Lena was a key to solving that mystery. She got close to Lena, exchanging mutual appreciation and affection, but found that under the surface was a sore point in Lena that could not be touched without an irrational hostility surfacing.

It was not until after the arrests that the Vista worker learned that Lena's group of thieves stole on order and had a garage full of stolen appliances as rewards to children who helped. Any youngster who wanted something for Mother's Day, Christmas, or birthday present went to the "traders" — as Lena's burglars called themselves — instead of to the Vietnam veteran's store. The traders had a simple pastoral-agricultural philosophy which they had developed to justify their thefts: "If you live near a woods full of pecan trees, you take all the pecans you can eat and you trade the rest of them for things you need."

Where were the city's pecan trees? The Vietnam veteran and other merchants had surplus goods which could be taken for trade. Lena, closely tied to a church she loved, had been one of the last young people in her housing project to accept the philosophy. She had not shared in the thefts until her family was forcibly moved by welfare officials from the old wooden apartment house they loved, which was close to school, church, shopping, and transportation and was inhabited by long-time residents who cared about each other. "Welfare" decided that the old apartments were a firetrap and moved Lena's mother to a new public housing project, far from their church and friends. Lena, age thirteen then, had not lived in the new project for a week before she was half-raped in the dark hall by a man looking for the prostitute next door; and she became friends with a dealer in stolen goods who was paying another woman on welfare for hiding him in her apartment.

Mother Josephine, Lena's Sunday School teacher, noticed that Lena was becoming a fighter, where previously she had been an almost perfect child. Lena quickly earned a leadership position among the youngsters who lived at the project because she could tear out a girl's earrings if attacked; and she could claw a boy's eyes with sharp fingernails. One boy said to Miss Eleanor, "If you see Lena get mad, call an ambulance."

Lena's First Theft

"What happened to her?" Mother Josephine asked.

The Vista worker explained that federal funds had been provided for summer jobs for teenagers from low-income families. People from the suburbs often say that "people on welfare won't work when they get the chance." Lena's older sister stood in line all night waiting for the employment office to open, but the next morning so many young people jammed inside, fighting for a chance to apply, that the dress Lena borrowed for her sister to wear was torn and ruined. Lena's sister was unable to pay for the dress because she didn't get a job. Lena's change and hostility began when a news-paper found that many of the jobs intended for the poor had gone instead to the children of middle-class politicians. The fact that the daughter of one alderman was Black, for example, made no differ-ence to welfare youngsters who learned that she was hired to supervise tennis courts in the park—paid to play tennis all summer, when her father earned over $30,000 a year.

Lena and her sister, meanwhile, proposed paying for the dress at a rate of fifty cents a week, but the girl whose dress had been ruined needed it to attend a wedding in three days. She took Lena to a department store to point out a dress she demanded as a replacement, saying, ". . . If you don't want a group-slapping-around-party this weekend, you better lift it."

Lena tried buying the dress on credit and offered to work for it at the store, explaining her crisis; but as she said to Miss Eleanor, "No one is human at a big store like that. They's just machines that's tuned only to say no, no, no, no . . ."

"Lena had no shoplifting experience, but she had friends who did, and they planned and executed a maneuvre which James Bond would have admired," Miss Eleanor said. Lena did not develop a taste for other such adventures, but the other youngsters who had helped her had problems too: welfare checks were lost or late, essential school supplies were lost or stolen from them with no money for replacement. At first Lena's gang stole only things that were desperately needed, and only from merchants who cheated the poor, or who refused to cash welfare checks or give credit. The Vietnam War veteran, Lena said, refused to give credit to people who were hungry and in trouble, so they stole from him until he was driven out of business. "In fact," Miss Eleanor said, "he felt the poor were better served by low prices which he could give only by refusing credit."

The man who had hidden in the apartment next door, admiring Lena's success, offered her an income which could take the family off welfare so they could move out of the much hated project. He would arrange to have a truck come to an abandoned garage every Thursday at 2:00 A.M. to load the merchandise which the youngsters had stolen—if they would concentrate on school equipment such as typewriters, musical instruments, for which "the fence" had a market in the South. Lena's arrest was a shock to the housing-project police who considered her to be the best influence in the neighborhood.

"She was!" Miss Eleanor said. "Lena was one of the last hold-outs in a project where every kid aged ten to twenty is involved in some kind of law breaking."

Who Gets Punished?

"Didn't Lena expect to get caught and punished?" I asked.

"Why should she?" Miss Eleanor replied, "when only one out of a hundred youngsters in her project ever gets caught. They all see it as a sort of lottery which is used by "them"—the establishment or society—to strike fear into the hearts of potential offenders. Every now and then a youngster is arbitrarily seized and is then punished as a scapegoat to set an example. The authorities may not publicly admit it, but they know that in the project one kid or another is arrested from time to time, whether guilty or innocent."

"But you said they are all guilty."

"And all are punished at one time or another. Lena thought she had had her turn when society punished her, when innocent, by moving her into the housing project; when she was almost raped, she asked over and over what she had done to deserve such punishment."

"So if arrest is entirely a matter of arbitrary chance, the threat of such punishment provides no reason to refrain from a particular crime?"

Miss Eleanor nodded. "At Lena's school the administration definitely has a policy of scapegoating. For example, pot keeps sneaking back into the building, first with smoking in the toilets, then in the halls, and finally some bold pupils try to smoke in class or gym. At this point the school authorities strike swiftly by seizing one or two offenders as an example, so as to drive the rest of the marijuana back into the street. Otherwise they feel they would soon have pushers selling it in the halls."

"But they wouldn't punish all the pot smokers?"

"No, the scapegoats are invariably the expendable youngsters, low on the totem pole. If the son of some politician got caught smoking pot in the restroom, he would somehow slip out of the net. If a dozen youngsters were caught, only two of them would be arrested. You see why Lena and her friends are hostile? By all the rules she should not have been made a scapegoat."

"Why was she?"

"Out-of-state police were involved in tracking down a big market in stolen school supplies. But Lena's friends continue to interpret all arrests as scapegoating and how the youngsters understand police behavior—even if incorrect—may be more influential than actual police behavior. For example, have you seen the project?"

"Ugly," I said. "Worse, I understand, than the slums that were torn down to build it."

Miss Eleanor agreed. "The contractor and architects are ashamed of it, saying that after the project was under construction the politicians forced them to skimp in ways that made decent housing impossible. A two-year-old boy was seriously injured there by a falling light fixture within a month of the project's opening. There are so many code violations in the construction and management that Vista workers aren't welcome there."

"What do they fear?"

"Not just exposure. Everyone 'knows' who was responsible for the violation of laws that are supposed to protect the poor. If you wonder why the people who live there are hostile to society, I suggest you try it for a few weeks."

"Weren't there arrests and fines after a legislative investigation of the project?"

Miss Eleanor laughed. "After the scapegoating? A contractor and one unpopular politician were made the fall guys with bad publicity and fines; and then they went out to break laws again just like the petty thieves in the lousy housing they built. Congress, of course, is guilty, in cutting back appropriations that had been promised to the city. There was supposed to be enough money for safe housing, where Lena wouldn't have been sexually attacked in the dark hall, but the Nixon administration diverted the funds elsewhere, leaving the contractor to be the scapegoat."

Court Punishment

"How will the court punish Lena?" I asked. She had confessed to being the mastermind of the school thefts.

"Severely," Miss Eleanor predicted. "The public is angry about burglaries, especially the theft of expensive musical instruments and shop machines. In theory the public wants all crimes punished equally; but, in fact, it gets more enraged about breaking-and-entering than about political graft that may do much more damage to society. Since Lena's adult accomplices will be tried in some southern state, she is needed as a scapegoat here after sensational newspaper stories about the ring. The police and establishment operate with two sets of rules. There is the myth which says, Get all the crooks and punish them severely; then there is an unwritten set of rules which are really applied—unless the newspapers or clergy get up in arms and demand that the authorities live up to the myth for a time. After her punishment Lena will return to her project to find nothing changed, much as the contractor will find little changed when he cooperates with the city on another building project. The difference is that Lena is concerned about her relationship with God because her mother and church friends care."

I tried to understand. "She's somehow being reconciled, where the contractor is not?"

"Oh, he's reconciled too, politically. The newspapers scapegoated him, using him to let the public discharge its anger over the graft of the guilty politicians; but once his fine was paid and his public humiliation was endured, he was given a contract to build another building. Society can't live by its myth because everyone is breaking laws, more so perhaps in Lena's neighborhood—but go look at the highways. What would happen if the police actually arrested all the guilty kids in The Corners?" She laughed. "The police, the courts, the detention center couldn't cope with so many kids at once, nor could they if all the grafting politicians were arrested at once! Society has to scapegoat."

"Don't they all get caught sooner or later?" I asked.

"Everyone dies sooner or later, but when a teenager gets terminal cancer he says, like Lena, Why me? You may not care for my cancer analogy, but doesn't the universe scapegoat?"

Miss Eleanor was wrong. Lena got a suspended sentence, partly because so many friends from her church went to court with her and promised to help her. Lena's mother said in court: "You punish a kid so she won't be bad again; but in this project everybody punishes without it workin' nohow. Maybe if we knew sooner, maybe if they always got bashed . . . but as it is, bashing only drives them out of the house and makes 'em sneaky so they don't talk anymore. Lord, I don't know. I know my Lena's going to turn out OK because church friends will keep her out of trouble. The Lord only knows if Lena can put all this bad stuff behind her, and if she come out not smelling too bad she'll work hard to make up for what she done. She's already helping Miss Eleanor with the block groups."

Where Lena is tall, with a sense of drama in her bearing, her mother is dumpy but has an infectious peace which the judge envied.

A clue: Sir Walter Moberly in *The Ethics of Punishment* (Hamden, Ct.: Shoe String Press, 1968) points out that society does not accidentally scapegoat but deliberately inflicts pain on the culprit who is caught to provide a dramatic lesson for everyone; a ritual which deliberately inflicts evil as a "kind of inverted sacrament" to provide a catharsis for society's anger. Many children live in a particularly dangerous world, according to Kenneth Kenniston of the Carnegie Council on Children. If Lena's apartment house was infected with disease, all children would be evacuated or quarantined until the place was completely safe. Doesn't the infection that exists in Lena's housing project provide an even greater danger to the children and to society? Such crimes cost society billions of dollars, yet the average citizen acts in the matter of juvenile crime as if such cancer can be cured by massive, uniform doses of castor oil.

IF HE IS GUILTY

The son of a well-known physician, his name not released by the court because he is a minor, was arrested Tuesday on charges of setting a series of "suspicious" fires in abandoned buildings more than twenty miles from his home.

The boy does not have a car.

The landlord of the buildings, Joseph X., committed suicide late last week when evidence for his culpability in the fires was presented to the grand jury.

The boy, whose friends say he was with them here at the time of the fires, has been released on bond to his parents for psychiatric examination. The court determined through preliminary medical examination that the boy was not a compulsive arsonist and was no danger to the community.

His teachers think it must be a mistake, his friends laugh at the charges, his parents have said that they will appeal as far as the Supreme Court to clear the family name.

If he's guilty, who were the other boys employed by the landlord? And why should a wealthy boy be sought out and employed for such dirty work? There must have been youngsters in the slum neighborhood who would have done it for less.

Suburban newspaper story

CHAPTER 7

Danny

"The risk of punishment makes it more exciting," Danny
said. *"Like poker when the stakes are high."*

"GOD IS GOOD for giving us malt and grape to make life exciting
until the big bang," Danny said as he toasted four teen-age friends
in a seedy back-road suburban bar, "so we can all get stinking
drunk for that grand finale when the whole world melts and burns."

Danny's cousin, G.V., a Harvard law student, said to me, "If
you want to talk to him to see his interpretation you must go to
the bar where he talks with his friends."

The boy is not yet sixteen. None of his friends are yet old
enough to drink legally, yet night after night you can find them in
a bar, getting drunk and plotting new criminal adventures, even
while Danny is on bail awaiting trial.

"On school nights too?" I asked.

"Yes, Danny was nearly six feet tall on his twelfth birthday and
he has been driving to bars with someone else's driving license
ever since he was thirteen."

"Don't his parents know?"

"What can they do?"

"Order him to stay home, at least on school nights," I said.

"They had to admit that they could no longer control Danny,
that they had no way to make him obey once he was thirteen.
You see, they wanted him to act grown-up; and Danny and his
friends drink and behave like adults in the bars. How could they
keep him at home when his mother withdraws with a sick headache

79

to get drunk—she is an alcoholic—and his father is always gone. He is a physician who has always said that he needs the relaxing atmosphere of the bar to unwind. He often took Danny to bars as a child, to 'let him see life as it is,' and Danny has used alcohol more or less regularly at home since he was five or six."

"Can't Danny's parents stop his allowance? Cut off his money?"

"No, his wealthy grandmother lavishes money on him to buy affection. I don't know how much she gives Danny but she sometimes sent me a hundred dollars a week when I was in high school—and she even sneaked it to me when my parents asked her not to do so."

"Then why did he burn down the buildings?" I asked. "Didn't his psychiatrist say that he did it for the money, that Danny is not a pyromaniac?"

"Danny's goal in life is excitement," G.V. explained, "and he and his gang are always looking for what he calls icing on the cake. They think it is fun, for example, to beat up a guy whom they suspect to be queer, to follow him out of the bar to a back alley and kick him in the balls a hundred times. That's what Danny calls 'cake.' But the cake is better with icing: it is more fun to kick if you are crazy-high. If you know the cops may come along and catch you . . . well, that's exciting. And if someone offered money if you would beat up the queer, that would add more icing to the cake."

"I don't understand."

"No one understands Danny! Let's go meet him so you can see for yourself. At the bar where he met the landlord who paid him for arson."

The young teenagers in the back corner of the bar welcomed us warmly because Danny likes and trusts his cousin. Danny also likes intelligent conversation on controversial topics. The son of a well-to-do surgeon, Danny has shaggy hair, a bulldog face, a lively sharp mind, a witty tongue and the manners of a politician. He spoke affectionately of his cousin who has spent a great deal of time on the legal and psychiatric aspects of Danny's forthcoming court case: "G.V., is a *nut* because he cares about me, about people, about the earth, the future. Once I was almost persuaded myself that the soil should be cherished, that people should be loved, that life was sacred. G.V. cares enough to do something, so I call him Pecan."

"Pecan?" one of his friends asked.

"He's not an *ordinary nut,* but one with real good meat inside. "I'm sorry about that little girl who got hurt in the fire I allegedly set." He nudged his lawyer cousin on the word *allegedly.* "But what does it matter if someone dies in a fire?"

"The Supreme Court says killing is OK," one of Danny's friends explained, referring to capital punishment.

Danny nodded. "We used to think it was OK only to kill our enemies in war, but now we build nuclear missiles to kill everyone, to blow up the whole damn earth. So why should I be punished for one little *alleged* fire?"

"Why is punishment exciting?" G.V. asked.

One of the other boys groaned. "The only time my old man ever comes alive and really looks at me is when Mom says I need punishing. Then sparks fly and life gets interesting."

"Sure," Danny said. "Who wants phony drama on TV when you can do more exciting things in real life."

"Cops and robbers?" G.V. asked.

"Sure," Danny replied.

"Real life cops are phony too," one of the other boys said. "They catch us racing 100 MPH down a narrow country road." He tried to imitate a tough cop: "You aren't sixteen, let me see your license, sonny. No license? Stolen car? You're driving while high? And your dad is president of the bank? Well, I'm going to . . ." The youngster giggled and tried to talk tougher, "I'm going to drive you right home and ask your dad to give you a good lecture!"

Danny interrupted, saying, "I've got the lecture memorized: 'Son, our family has a certain position in this community, one that is important for the business, so I must warn you that if you ever again are caught driving a stolen car while drunk . . . I'm going to . . . I'm going to . . .'"

"Make you be home by 2:00 A.M. on school nights, at least until you're fifteen years old!"

"No!" Danny protested to his friend, "we don't want him at home playing that damn stereo all night!"

"Cut off his allowance."

"No, then he'll steal our liquor and sell it to his friends."

"Holy Spirits! The Comforter!"

Danny stood dramatically to point a finger at himself. "Son, if you ever embarrass this family again, I'm going to . . ." He raised his voice to a more dramatic pitch, "I'm going to . . . speak to your mother!"

The boys laughed hilariously.

"He wouldn't dare do that," one of his friends said. "She . . . might speak back. She might say she wants a divorce, and the property settlement would be so complicated!"

"I want to talk to you about punishment," I said.

"Why," Danny asked, "is that what you most enjoy? Are you a disciple of the wicked Marquis (De Sade) who wants to spend your last days savoring the pain delights of others?"

"You enjoy punishment?" G.V. asked him.

"Of course not," Danny retorted. "But it is the danger that makes it exciting, the risk of danger. It's fun to scale a cliff or drive fast or to parachute . . . but it's the danger that is the icing on the cake."

"And excitement *is all there is* to life in the last days," one of Danny's friends added.

Danny explained, "We live here in the shadow of a nuclear plant which could blow up at any moment. You ask why I don't join the clam shellers who agitate to shut it down? Why bother? It's the first firecracker on a fuse which is going to blow the whole damn world up, any day now."

One of the tipsy boys said, "The earth is in the hands of an angry God."

"Or maybe a God of justice," Danny said, "who lets stupid people get what they deserve. Now what would you do if you had only an hour to live?" He looked around at his friends. "Make love? Drink with your friends?"

As if on cue the four boys raised their beer cans to drink. This group of teenagers, G.V. told me, had been carrying on a serious dialogue about the future of humanity for several years, but by the time they were fourteen they had talked themselves into complete despair: their families and schools were useless, empty, even ridiculous. All they had was this drinking fellowship and camaraderie with each other. Hungry for family life they have never known, they had become family to each other. Danny now cares for nothing else but these friends. Only they have the power to punish him so that he would feel it. Only their interpretation of any experience, including that of punishment, can be heard by Danny. If they think that all there is to life is drinking together, they have learned it in their homes.

One of Danny's teachers said the same thing: "It may be that Danny's parents, his church, his school have some values, some hope, some faith, but Danny doesn't see such modeled in the lives of anyone he cares about. His parents would be very angry to hear me say this, but I think Danny lives up to the best he sees in his parents' lives, to the best he ever hears from them—although, of course, most of what he has seen and heard at home has been on TV. Danny is a product of the TV age. He's the Sesame-Street kid who must be continually entertained with something new and exciting all the time."

"I want to know how Danny has been punished at school."

My question startled the teacher. "Anyone who raised a hand to Danny would be sued, or fired for lacking creative imagination in handling a problem."

"Then Danny is a problem at school?"

"No. If Danny comes to school a bit high, then the class conversation will be more lively and interesting. He and his friends are gracious and disarming in their contempt for teachers. They are polite to us, as to servants. They are artists at manipulating and disarming adults, even the police. The cops tried to be stern with Danny when they arrested him, but Danny's jokes kept them laughing. They couldn't help it."

"Danny joked?"

"He loved every minute of it, as if after years of watching TV, he was finally on camera himself. Just watch how he dramatizes everything and enjoys the drama."

School Punishment

"If Danny hasn't been punished much at school," the teacher added, "it's partly because we saw early that he wanted punishment—or enjoyed the risk of punishment—so we determined not to play that game."

I was tempted to ask the teacher what games they did like to play at school. When I asked Danny whether he had ever been punished at school, he replied, "Oh yes. It is grim what the headmaster does to you if, for example, you bring a gun to school and shoot a teacher."

"Or after being late three mornings in a row," another boy added.

"The headmaster would call you in for a lecture . . ." Danny said.

"Standing," another boy interrupted.

"Oh yes, he would stand there and keep you standing for a while . . . looking deep into your eyes with disappointment."

"Disappointment, such disappointment," one of the others said.

"Then the headmaster would clear his throat slowly and say, 'Paulk, I understand that shooting a teacher could be an accident, *but you must be punished for being late three days in a row.'*"

"No! No!" the other boys protested. One said, "The headmaster would say, 'Paulk, since this is the first time you ever killed anyone, we will just put you on warning that you'll be suspended if you ever shoot another teacher. But you know the rules about being late for coffee! So for the next three days I want you to report to the chaplain for discipline.'"

"The chaplain is the punishment officer?"

"Discipline," Danny replied. "The old chaplain who was with the school for fifty years used to punish boys by making them memorize psalms, but this one . . ."

"Who has been chaplain for only thirty years," another interrupted.

Danny imitated the voice of a tottering old man: "This chaplain believes, with Browning, that there is no hope for the criminal, 'save in such a suddenness of fate' that the 'truth may be flashed out in one blow.' " Danny suspended the drama for a moment to say, condescendingly, "From the *Ring and The Book.*"

One of the other boys added, "The chaplain punishes you by making you listen to such poetry, but he coughs so much between words that you can escape the punishment . . . by listening to the coughs instead of to the words."

"Doesn't sound severe," I said.

"He spreads germs when he coughs," Danny explained. "And

after listening (cough) to lines about the night's black (cough) and the blaze of thunder (cough) striking blow on blow (cough) . . . you have to go through the belt line, especially for bringing pills to school."

"Belt line?" I asked. "Corporal punishment?"

"You're an acorn if you think that," Danny replied. "Going through the belt line means apologizing to every damn functionary of the school: "I'm sorry, Mr. Tennis Court Attendant, sir, that my behavior has not been worthy of the honorable traditions of St. Judas' School."

The boys all laughed and another one tried to continue the drama, saying, "And I know, sir, Mr. Soccer Team Bus Driver, that our school has a certain position in this community, that it is important for business, and I don't want to embarrass the school so I promise never to be late for coffee again, at least not when I come to shoot a teacher."

The boys jokingly argued about which teacher ought to be shot first while G.V. and I discussed the complexity of Danny's personality, his family experience, and his milieu. I listened to the boys with one ear when I heard one of them say, "Whenever my old man hears that I've been speeding it makes him so mad that he drives all over town at 90 MPH, hunting for me."

"What would he do if you shot a teacher?" another asked.

Danny's eyes grew wide with excitement. "Maybe the electric chair. Wouldn't that be great? All the TV people waiting around, phoning the governor about a reprieve, then the tense moment when the executor actually pulls the switch."

G.V., as an attorney, interrupted, "I think you mean 'executioner' rather than executor and I don't think you would like the chair as much as you think."

"Oh man!" Danny protested. "What else is left? Just think of the excitement when they would ask if I had any last words, and I would say, 'Yeah, these guys,'" he pointed around the table to his friends, "'have rigged it up electronically so that when the electrocutor pulls the switch the atomic power plant will also blow up . . . boom . . .'"

His friends all cheered.

"We've tried everything else to get high," Danny continued, "drugs, sex, alcohol, fires, so the next thing we have got to figure out is some way to raid and explode that nuclear power station. We might be asleep when it blows up otherwise, and miss that beautiful foretaste of Armageddon."

Home Punishment

"If you had a child," I asked Danny, "how would you punish him?"

"Oh he'd have to be punished, wouldn't he, to teach him not to run out into the street in front of cars. So I'd punish him just like other parents do. I'd leave the helpless little child alone in front of the TV set, hour after hour."

One of the other boys snarled, "Child abuser!"

Danny nodded. "You're right, that's child abuse. But if you take away my whip and TV, how else could I punish?" He thought for a moment, wrinkling his forehead as he replied seriously, "All the world's a stage so, punishment or reward, it's all in the drama. How can we take the culprit out of the ordinary relations of humanity and enclose him in a sphere by himself so that he can sorrow in reverence over what he has done, over what has seared his inmost heart."

I was impressed, thinking that the words and thoughts were Danny's until his friends applauded. Then he added, again condescendingly, "Hawthorne, *Scarlet Letter.* Or do you prefer Freud on punishment?" He lowered his voice to a whisper. "Our Marxist Freudian Episcopal faculty is always embarrassed to speak of God because they've lost all sense of drama and how can you punish unless you see it as a play?"

"Punishment as drama?"

"A solemn initiation into the mystery of mystical meaning for those who believe in God. For the others," he waved his hand around the table of friends, "there is no heaven, no hell, no punishment, no beginning, no end . . ."

"But your parents tried to punish you," G.V. said to Danny.

"When my father tried to play God," Danny replied, "he appeared on stage as half-Shylock and half-Mickey-Mouse. As for my mom, she used to try to punish me for drinking when I was in the first grades of school, but usually she wasn't sober enough. I mean, she couldn't really make herself do it without drinking, so whenever she was hot on the A.A. she would give up punishing me too." He winced a moment as he added, "That meant she gave up on me, too."

"It's true," G.V. said to me privately. "They gave up on Danny. If they didn't know how to punish him, he sure knew how to punish them! By exposing every raw nerve in their fragile relationship with each other and with him. Danny lived pretty much with the TV set until he was old enough, ten or eleven, to go out with his friends. He grew up then, perhaps at too young an age, because he found with his peers the emotional support and relationships he needed and didn't find at home. As many middle-class or upper middle-class surburban youngsters, Danny became an adult at thirteen and his family lost all control. They couldn't accept the fact, or understand it, or punish him out of it. They realized, unconsciously perhaps, that they had to let him go. Unable to establish an adult relationship with so young a child, they abandoned him psychologically and emotionally."

"Abandon is a strong word," I said, "to apply to 'many families in the suburbs' as you do."

"Danny began at eleven and twelve to have deep, meaningful conversations with these friends, where his parents talked with each other and their friends only on a chitty-chatty superficial level."

"Surely they tried to talk to Danny," I said.

"Like my parents, they perhaps didn't even know how to create a community of common interests and conversation. When Danny's father or my dad 'sat us down for a talk' that usually meant a lecture or a scolding. We had to turn away from our parents for dreams and hopes and ideas and intellectual adventures. The family dialogue which was needed to nurture personality and relationships was unintentionally a punishing one, partly because our parents really never listened."

"Danny's father was a busy physician," I said.

G.V. retorted angrily, "Danny's father doesn't even know how to listen to his patients, only how to lecture them. Listening is a skill he never learned, which may be why his wife became an alcoholic." He paused for a moment, then added, "Maybe as a physician he couldn't talk about medical problems with a nine-year-old boy so he went off to the bar to drink."

"Not with his wife?"

"Heavens no," G.V. laughed. "Encourage an alcoholic wife? That would be as peculiar as staying at home to listen to a ten-year-old son's ponderous theories about the imminent collapse of Western civilization. Danny wrote a paper about the economic, political, nuclear, and ecological collapse of civilization in the fifth grade. He showed it to his father, perhaps the boy's last desperate effort to have a serious conversation with his father, who put it aside, saying he would read it when he got time."

"And never read it?"

"No, so Danny angrily wrote another paper about 'forbidden pleasures' outlining a series of experiences that a kid might seek for amusement while waiting for the world to blow up. He didn't show that version to his dad because he couldn't think of anything shocking enough; but he and his friends are still working on it, and by now they have a list that would make the hair on the back of your head sizzle. They were bored with drugs, alcohol, and sex before they were out of junior high; then they tried stealing cars, breaking into houses, vandalizing people's expensive art objects as a joke. They've literally played with dynamite, making home-made bombs. They've tried torture, on animals and people, and they've set fire to buildings. What next?"

"And Danny really has found his arrest and all that goes with it exciting?"

"He has enjoyed every moment of it as drama, especially the impact on his parents, who, he feels, have been forced to pay some attention to him again."

"Masochism?"

"Words are tricky," G.V. replied. "I knew an old man who enjoyed dying. He saw his inevitable death, as Danny views his court punishment, as another of life's interesting experiences. There is some pain, maybe, but Danny experiences that like the skier who barely notices the cold, stinging wind as he sails down the mountainside."

"But when he crashes at the bottom?"

"I don't know. Danny may find prison to be another interesting experience, another drama to live out. Of course Danny is confi-dent—and he may be right—that he will never go to jail. His father has lots of money for appeal after appeal, for years on end."

"Would it all be as exciting without the alcohol?"

G.V. raised his hands. "It is difficult to imagine what anything would be like in Danny's home and community without alcohol, the socially-accepted drug to soothe all pains."

When we were alone in the car Danny said to G.V., "It's funny that I asked you to take me home, because the bar is really my home, and our house is a sort of bar." Then unexpectedly he turned to me and said, "You know, maybe I care more about Mom and Dad than they care about me. Have you talked to them about me?"

"They won't see me," I said.

"Of course not. You said you wanted to talk about punishment? You think my mom is going to tell you how she used to get mad at me when I was a little kid. It didn't take much to get her drunk, you know. She already had alcohol in her veins, instead of blood, when I was born. The neighbors called the cops once, when I was a year old. I'm not supposed to know about it, but the cops found her in a stupor and me lying in the blood where she fell."

"Blood?"

"Never on purpose! But that's why we moved out here, you know. They'll tell you the city was dangerous for kids, lousy schools, muggings. But they moved because the neighbors lived too close and knew all about her. How she made me cry by screaming at me and scolding me all the time."

"Sometimes Danny was scared to death of her," G.V. explained.

"But I was smart," Danny continued. "When people on TV yelled like Mom it was exciting. So I pretended she was a mad queen, or a witch, or a demon, or goblin, or ghost and that made it more exciting. If she punished me by locking me in my room I would climb out the third-story window and hang there until she had to call the fire department to 'rescue' me."

Danny's psychiatrist said to me later, "I don't know how to explain it, but Danny persuaded himself—and his parents—even before he was old enough to go to school that he enjoyed being punished.

"The drama of it," I said.

"Well, more than that. It's true that he somehow turned every effort they made to punish him into an adventure. His vivid imagination could make it terribly exciting, as when he would pretend he was being chased by beautiful girls. You may not believe this, but Danny's father says they gave up because the only way he could successfully punish his son was to refuse to punish him. And his father is a physician and a very intelligent man."

"And a good father?" I asked.

The psychiatrist smiled blandly. "It would not be professional of me to pass judgment on that." He wiped his chin. "But I can say that he is a competent enough physician to have learned a great deal from fifteen years of mistakes with Danny."

"Enough to become reconciled with Danny?"

"Danny and his father had a two-hour conversation about world politics," the psychiatrist replied, "while waiting to see a busy lawyer recently. Both of them were astonished to discover that the other had intelligent things to say."

"About the end of the world?"

"No, about Danny's mother and her need for both of them. Danny cried a little and said, 'Dad, maybe the three of us could be together when the world blows up?' "

A clue: Dr. Rodney Shapiro finds that violence "is best understood not as the isolated act of a single individual but as an eruption traceable to complex relationships within the family," (according to Lawrence van Gelder's "Family Violence: Another View," New York Times. May 29, 1979). Shapiro finds that "most . . . behavioral disturbances are a reflection of disturbed interpersonal relationships within a family system," a departure from traditional psychiatric training which locates the source of disturbed behavior within the individual. Seymour Halleck in Psychiatry and the Dilemmas of Crime (Berkeley: University of California Press, 1971) discusses how some people enjoy being punished.

Another clue: Clifton Fadiman ("The Classroom's Ubiquitous Rival: Pop Culture," New York Times. June 13, 1979) points out that for the first time in history a child must be a citizen of two competing cultures: the tradition he meets at school and the media's counter-culture; and two reality systems, one of which expounds the religion of instantaneous sensation, gratification, and excitement.

BOY ARRESTED FOR BRUTAL TRAIN DEATH

Police this morning arrested a fourteen-year-old juvenile charged with the senseless murder of an elderly derelict who fell under the wheels of a train yesterday, allegedly kicked there during a teen-age fight. The arrested juvenile has run away from correctional institutions so many times that authorities have lost count and was supposed to be in court facing charges of dealing in heroin at the time of the murder. He has a record of continual truancy, vagabondage, incorrigibility, and petty offenses since age nine.

The prosecutor is asking that the boy be sent to the state reformatory, pending trial, because there is no juvenile facility secure enough to hold him. The fourteen-year-old was allegedly trying to push an older boy under the train, Alfonso X., who said that the arrested boy had been calling him vile names. The two boys had previously known each other in the juvenile detention center.

From the back page of a metropolitan newspaper

CHAPTER 8

Wisher

"It makes no sense at all," Wisher said. *"They punish you if you do or if you don't. If you cut school they lock you up where there's no school, and if you're bad they put you in a place that makes you worse."*

"WHAT SORT OF A MONSTER would do something like that?" Horrified by the senselessness when a teenager shoves an innocent person in front of a train, people not only invariably ask that question, but in Wisher's case a petition was circulated demanding the electric chair for the fourteen-year-old. Indignation was high because Wisher was also charged with selling cocaine and heroin to school children as young as ten and with recruiting children from the best schools to sell drugs; and he had been in and out of jail so many times that the petition suggested that he should be listed in the *Guiness Book of World Records*.

One legislator used Wisher in a fiery speech in favor of changing state laws so that such "vicious juvenile criminals could be locked away for twenty years."

Not yet tried or sentenced, Wisher was in a maximum-security reformatory because, from age eleven, he had shown an almost unbelievable genius at escaping from custody. He had, for example, walked out of the detention center right in front of two officers who later joked that Wisher must have the ability to make himself invisible.

Al Carter, the court social worker who took me to meet the boy, was a long-haired man of twenty-four who talked with a lisp

and had bad teeth. "Why do you want to see such shit?" he
asked me. "Wisher's not really American and won't talk to anyone
but his weird priest. I'll take you along but don't be surprised
if the monster turns out to be a scared little bunny rabbit!"

Wisher was brought to a reformatory classroom by two guards
who grinned but said nothing as they unfastened the handcuffs.
He was of average size for a fourteen-year-old, had black hair,
a creamy white complexion from being locked up so much in
solitary confinement for punishment, and would even have been
handsome if he hadn't looked so washed out and his eyes so
empty. The youngster refused to speak even when Carter tried
taunting him, shaming him with false accusations, making promises
to take him out of solitary if he would talk.

"Why is Wisher being punished in solitary?" I asked.

'He's not being punished," the social worker replied. "He's
much younger and weaker than other inmates here, so he is in
segregation for his own protection."

"Not punished?" I checked my notes. "Last week he spent three
nights in a punishment cell with no mattress."

"Technically that isn't punishment," Carter explained. "Runaways are locked up alone for a time 'to give them a chance to
think things over,' so they will decide to be more cooperative.
There was no restraint, no withholding of food."

"No restraint? What about the handcuffs?"

"He's just being held pending trial, but he's so clever at running
away that he has to be handcuffed when he's not in his cell.
If he would communicate with us, would cooperate, he wouldn't
ever have been in the detention center the first time four years
ago. If he would only have been willing to give the cops his name
and address! They had no alternative with a stubborn runaway
kid, in the middle of the night, but to take him to the shelter
until we could find out who he was and take him home. He was
not being punished at all."

When I reported the conversation to Father Gregorius, he
blushed and his eyes burned with anger. "Not punished at all?"
He was especially angry to read what court workers like Carter had
written in Wisher's file.

"Wisher's mother speaks such poor English that she only pre-
tends to understand what such officials say. She is such a gracious

lady that they leave her apartment feeling that none of it is her fault. She was an aristocrat in her own country, before coming here as a refugee, and she never learned how to cook, to clean house, to care for children. Even on welfare she expects someone else to wait on her. One child after another rebelled and left home, but Wisher was the good one who stayed to cook, to clean, to care for the babies."

I touched the boy's file. "Meanwhile getting this reputation for delinquency from cutting school . . ."

"His mother charms school authorities like a princess," the priest went on. "She tells them that she sacrifices everything, that she is trying to get Wisher to go to school; then the next morning she weeps and begs Wisher to stay home to clean the kitchen because she's too sick even to make her own tea."

"Is she ill?"

"Quite weak, perhaps. She was born frail and was sickly as a child; but since coming to America much of her illness is psychological; she pines for own country or her servants there, even though she knows that she can never return with a Marxist government in power. And she has been sick over her husband's total failure as an artist in America. He has hardly earned a cent and comes home several times a year to borrow money from his wife's welfare check until he can find another patroness. They have a passionate reunion every time he returns. Twelve children! I do not doubt that they love each other very much and that he would have been a good husband in his own country; but here he finds one silly woman after another who feeds him and beds him while he paints her portrait and that of her friends. What a sad life for the son of a distinguished statesman: a gigolo!"

"They say that he is sweet and shy like Wisher."

"Yes, and as easy to overlook. Wisher always seems surprised when someone glances at him, as if he never expected others to recognize that he was really there. He didn't speak a word of English when he entered school, nor was there anyone within shouting distance of his school who understood a Slavic language. So teachers assumed for six years that his only learning disability, his failure to learn to read, was the result of his poor grasp of English, in addition to what they perceived as a stubborn unwillingness to talk or learn English."

I opened his file. "It now seems that Wisher can't read because no one recognized his dyslexia, i.e., he sees his letters upside down and backwards."

"Wisher came to hate school," Father Gregorius said, "because he couldn't read like the others and didn't know why. He refused to speak at school to hide his ignorance. At school he pretended not to understand English; and at home, when asked what was wrong at school, he replied in English which his mother didn't understand. His brothers and sisters, who did well in school, brought home the word that 'Wisher was dumb.' If he couldn't read in either language, then why shouldn't he stay home to take care of a sick mother and babies? They made no conscious decision to turn Wisher into a domestic, but the other children had after-school jobs and Wisher was sweet and willing to stay home, since the housework was all he ever got praised for! And he enjoyed taking care of his younger brothers and sisters, who gave him affection. It was several years before he realized he had fallen into a trap, working at home from morning to night seven days a week."

Wisher taught his mother to wash vegetables when he was in the third grade. Earlier she had cooked them without removing the dirt or rot. He also took over changing the babies because she did it only once a day and sometimes quieted them with drugs when they cried.

"He got the name Wisher," the priest explained, "because he was a dreamer who began every sentence with *I wish*. He wished his daddy would come home, he wished he could read, he wished his mother would get well, he wished to be at school when he was at home, and at home when he was at school, he wished he could run away like his brothers. I have a large parish; people scattered over three counties. Whenever I went to Wisher's home his mother met me with imperious demands to come more often to help her. I didn't learn until later that she often hid Wisher when school authorities came."

Father Gregorius warned the social agency that Wisher would soon start running away from home, and a new young welfare worker—impressed with Wisher's mother, her bearing and manners—called him an interfering priest.

"She told me to take care of religion and she would take care of Wisher. Well, where was she the next year when Wisher was on the streets all night? I learned my lesson too late. I should have fought the system for him as his friend."

I asked Father Gregorius how Wisher had been punished at home.

"Hardly at all! His mother never disciplined her children. She would dissolve into tears if they didn't do exactly what she wanted. She would sob until Wisher would promise her just about anything."

"Didn't the welfare people see that she was exploiting Wisher?"

"Evidently not. They were more concerned that she was behind with her rent and grocery bills and she told everyone that Wisher was a liar and thief. I'm sure she didn't realize she was giving him a bad reputation. It was her older children who stole everything she had of value. Maybe she thought Wisher did it too. Wisher followed his brothers to the street, whenever he could, trying to earn some money shining shoes. She was humiliated to have her children shine shoes, but Wisher was the only one she pursued. She would send the police after him to get him home in time to cook supper. She was therefore responsible for his first arrests and for making the neighborhood police believe that Wisher was a delinquent and thief. The juvenile court began to warn him, when he was nine and ten, that if he kept running away he would be sent to the state reform school."

Unauthorized Punishment

"But his first incarceration resulted from being picked up by the police in a far corner of the city late at night?"

"Wisher was terrified and refused to give his name. He ran away, was caught and returned to the detention center where he . . ." Father Gregorius blushed, unable to speak directly about the way ten-year-old Wisher had been sodomized, raped by a gang of older toughs at the center. "You want to know why Wisher fled, time after time?" He showed me some well-worn clippings from New York City newspapers, describing the detention center at the time Wisher was first there:

New York Times: " . . . a house of horror . . . children harm each other . . . violent assaults, rapes, fights with knives, chains, glass . . . forced homosexuality common . . . the use of alcohol and drugs rampant . . . The center has recently been plagued by a doubling

of successful escapes . . . a school guard arrested for raping a
juvenile inmate . . ."

New York Daily News: ". . . cocaine smuggled into the institution . . . One youth passed out after an overdose of heroin . . .
Youngsters of 10 or 12 sent to sleep in dorms with 16- and 17-year-
old drug addicts and murderers . . . beaten for refusing to submit
to the sexual advances of older boys . . . Such youngsters often
there only for truancy."

Village Voice: ". . . I have witnessed numerous cases of physical
abuse of boys forced into homosexual relations . . . torn rectal
areas . . . emotional or moral impairment . . . brutal beatings . . .
One youngster whose eyesight was impaired by a brutal assault . . .
no medical attention for a week . . ."

Father Gregorius pounded his fist on the table. "And they punish
Wisher for running away like a scared rabbit? What horrifies me
even more is, as you can see in his file, that the court considered
him more and more delinquent, more and more criminal, simply
for running away in an effort to escape rape and abuse. If Wisher
came home his mother called the police, telling him that he must
never hide from the authorities. She actually thought that a few
days in the correctional institution would 'be good for him,' would
teach him to stay home and help her."

Wisher learned about "the magic man" in the correctional
institution. The nickname charmed Wisher even before he saw the
drug dealer's humorous magic tricks, and the jailed youngsters
told wild tales of wealth and pleasures the magic man could
provide. Fearing to go home, the runaway sought out the magic
man for a job, and went to work carrying messages, delivering
contraband cigarettes — a cover for marijuana.

"If you want to know why a boy like Wisher starts using drugs,"
Father Gregorius said, "it's for the magic! Wisher says that the
first time he used pot he felt as if it was what he had been
waiting for all his life. Kids use pot, I guess, for the same reason
their parents use sleeping pills and alcohol. Do you know the
essay by Vasily Vasilyevich Rozanov, *Sweet Jesus and the Sour
Fruits of the World*? He shows how people can be satisfied with

quite tasteless bread until they get a taste of better, heavenly bread. Some kids don't know how empty their lives are. When Wisher's father came home their house was brightened with music, art, the rich traditions of a great family. At the holy liturgy when the gospel shone forth Wisher also sensed the sourness of the earth's fruits; his own life was flat and tasteless."

I struggled to understand. "Many youngsters are inspired to work in school when they discover possibilities in life . . ."

"I became aware of something in Wisher that had to explode," the priest continued, "when he confessed . . . there was something that had to become violent or be artistically transformed."

Father Gregorius cleared his schedule for three days when the boy was twelve to try to straighten out Wisher's life. He went first to the detention center; there he was referred to the court, then to a new case worker who couldn't find Wisher's file and didn't phone back as she had promised. "I will say in her defense that I found her in the hospital with appendicitis," the priest said. "But there was a two-week delay in passing his file on to someone else, while Wisher was suffering terribly in jail. I went to a children's rights group to ask for money and a lawyer, but like the detention center they were short of money and staff. I can't really blame any of those over-worked people. That juvenile jail doesn't get enough money from the legislature for staff enough to keep the older inmates from running it on a 'bully system.' Everyone kept putting me off, saying they were trying to get his school records straightened out."

"But you did get Wisher out and into a foster home," I said.

"To a good place with one of our church families, but Wisher's mother had him home again in six weeks, having persuaded the social agency that 'she needed him.' By law a mother's rights to a child take priority, unless the court acts to take him from the home."

Wisher's school records were muddled and inaccurate. It was almost impossible to find a teacher who would accept any responsibility for him, until—in another school district while he was in the foster home—he fell into the hands of a reading teacher who discovered his dyslexia and began to make some progress teaching him to read with some new experimental materials. Until then,

most teachers had ignored Wisher as a silent refugee child who
spoke poor English and "had no motivation."

"Wisher was eager to read," Father Gregorius said. "He and I
were both delighted to find that his problem was seeing letters
upside down. When his mother took him out of the foster home
and he went back to his old school he tried to tell the teachers
about the new materials and his dyslexia. He brought along an
explanatory letter from the reading specialist . . ."

"And his teachers refused to try the experimental materials?"

"Worse than that! They were forbidden to do so because no
'unapproved materials' could be used."

"Surely an exception could be made," I suggested.

"Oh, if Wisher's mother had been the type to go to the school and
scream . . . but Wisher soon ran away again. So I intervened with
the social agency and for once they acted . . . but you could almost
write a comedy about what happened next. A court social worker
took Wisher to a special school where the principal asked her to
take the boy to a remedial reading class—with the materials and
instructions. The social worker, perhaps misunderstanding the room
number, dropped Wisher off at the wrong room. The teacher
in the 'wrong class,' not knowing where Wisher was supposed to be,
gave him a note to return to the office. To Wisher, 'going to
the office' meant punishment. Scared, unable to read the note, he
simply left school by the nearest exit. He spent the rest of the
day looking for the 'magic man' for help to go back to the 'good
school' near his foster home."

When Wisher was arrested for truancy and drug peddling, no
one blamed or even informed the principal or the teachers at
the special school. The fault, according to the court, was entirely
Wisher's.

"It never occurred to me," Father Gregorius said, "to check
Wisher's record, which—as you can see—says that he lied about
the reason for walking out of the special school. You see where
someone wrote across the page, 'Chronic liar, sexual deviant,
completely undependable, must be kept institutionalized.' Maybe
Wisher did lie, but I tell you he was deceived and lied to a
thousand times first. His court record says that he lied about
being sexually abused at the detention center. Is that there to

protect negligent staff? Or because other inmates lied to protect themselves? Without proper investigation, at age twelve, he was labeled a sexual deviant."

"Is he homosexual?"

Response to Punishment

"Absolutely not! Wisher was terribly hurt and angry at the suggestion. Indeed, that's why he accidentally pushed the crippled man into the train, and why he broods so sullenly and refuses to talk to anyone now in the reformatory. He knows that he is kept in seclusion because he has 'a certain reputation'—completely undeserved since the sexual involvement with other inmates was forced upon him against his will."

"How did it happen?" I asked. "How did he knock the man under the train?"

The priest looked sad. "I wish I could say it was an accident. Wisher was blind with rage when he saw Alphonso, an older boy who had raped him several times in the detention center, and was now spreading rumors in the neighborhood that Wisher was 'a queer.' I was scared of what I saw in Wisher's eyes when he told me about it and said, "I'll show him I'm a man!" Alphonso and his friends taunted Wisher as soon as he came into the station, yelling, 'Fag! Fag!' Wisher blushed and fled, but halfway up the steps he turned around and ran toward Alphonso as if he was to tackle him in football. I'm not sure what happened next, because Wisher doesn't remember for sure either. The crippled man egged on the older boys who were trying to pull off Wisher's pants in public, and, somehow, although Wisher's arms were held, he kicked at the drunken derelict, causing the man to fall in front of the train. I truly believe that is the truth, although Alphonso and his friends told a story to the police that completely exonerated them of any wrong-doing."

Alphonso and the other boys signed sworn statements that Wisher attacked them and the crippled man unexpectedly, and for no reason.

"So what will the court do with Wisher?" I asked.

The priest hit the table again. "His mother has agreed to an indeterminate sentence, which means that the boy should be incarcerated until he 'settles down.' She was horrified by Wisher's arrest for manslaughter . . . more so than for drug peddling. I have some hope for Wisher, however. I hope we can get him out of the reformatory into a camp where he can do some gardening. He dreams of saving money for a greenhouse. He wants to experiment with growing vegetables in chemicals. Although I have brought him organic gardening magazines and catalogs, it mystifies me how a boy who can't read could already know so much about that. Maybe he can survive several years of incarceration because he's beginning to assert himself. The moment he turned on the stairs to go back and attack Alphonso for slandering him, for making false accusations about his morality and character, Wisher ceased being a helpless youngster in a trap."

"So perhaps he is finding another magic to replace the fantasies he has when high on drugs?"

"I'm recruiting volunteers to read to him, to share in his growing interest in gardening. Now, if I can find people who share that interest and are willing to visit him, and willing to help him find a job working in truck farming when he gets out."

Three months later, when Wisher's petition to go to a farm camp was denied by the court because of his reputation as an escapee, Wisher tied knots in his sheet to make a rope to hang himself.

A clue: Patricia Wald in "Trying a Juvenile Right-to-Treatment Suit" (*American Journal of Criminal Law.* Summer, 1974) reports the "double-talk" and "double-think" practiced by the juvenile justice system as in the punishment by whippings, hard labor detail, and strip cells of youngsters like Wisher, not yet tried and found guilty. As in Wisher's case, such punishments are frequently justified as "good for the child" and "to give him time to think things over." A research report on "the overcrowding and dehumanization in correctional facilities" (*Behavior Today.* Sept. 12, 1977) concludes: "the juvenile justice system is in a state of progressive breakdown . . . with states giving it little attention." Citizens must take political action.

Another clue: Edward Wynne of the College of Education, University of Illinois at Chicago Circle (*New York Times.* Jan. 17,

1976), speaks of our current process as encouraging the young to brutalize each other. ". . . Serious punishment and love should be inextricably intermingled," he writes. "I believe the decline of deliberate *significant* punishment—as compared to the punishment of bureaucratic indifference—is related to the decline of caring and love."

Those who feel that we have loaded our case by selecting such interesting youngsters should be reminded that every human being is intriguingly interesting if one finds a way to get inside his or her story.

At that time, the disciples came to Jesus saying, "Who is greatest in the kingdom of heaven?"
And calling to him a child, he put him in the midst of them and said, "Truly I say to you . . . whoever receives one such child in my name receives me; but whoever causes one of these little ones to sin, it would be better for him to have a great millstone fastened around his neck and to be drowned in the depth of the sea . . . See that you do not despise these little ones."

Part Two

*How
Were They Reconciled?*

CHAPTER 9

Common Sense

NO ONE YET KNOWS how laws and social institutions must change to provide long-range effective solutions to juvenile crime: welfare reform? comprehensive health care including psychotherapy funds? educational reform? comprehensive family services? changes in courts and prisons? It seems unlikely that the justice system will be effectively changed before the year 2000.

Meanwhile, you and I must do what we can on the basis of common sense. For example, if a child's artery is cut, it is common sense to apply a tourniquet and to hug and comfort the child while waiting for the physicians to arrive.

The second half of this book suggests some things that communities can begin to do about crime while waiting for the system to change. An illustration of interim common-sense action is suggested by a newspaper editorial which says that "neighborhoods are engulfed by a flood of juvenile crime." It makes sense, when there is a flood, to boil the water and sandbag the homes while waiting for the experts to bring long-range solutions such as typhoid shots and flood-control dams. While we wish to encourage and support the professionals, what we propose here is addressed to the amateurs, the lovers of children: ordinary citizens, parents, church members, volunteers. There are ways we can "hug" and "boil water" and "sandbag homes" that can do a great deal to prevent juvenile crime simply by seeking to establish one-to-one relationships with troubled and problem youngsters.

The stories of these seven juveniles suggest two helpful kinds of common-sense action which can be undertaken by ordinary people in any sort of neighborhood. First, we can try to find out what is actually going on in punishment—in homes, schools, courts—and experiment with some ways to improve its effectiveness; and second, we can involve ourselves in the process of healing after punishment, that is, in bringing punishment to the point of effective completion.

Punishment and Reconciliation

Any good parent knows that punishment—of any kind—has little long-range constructive effect *unless the offender is afterwards forgiven, reconciled,* and welcomed back into the warmth of the family circle with self-respect and dignity. American society has not yet found how to reconcile tens of thousands of youngsters, who therefore, get caught up in criminal underworlds, subcultures, or gangs in search of the relationships which can heal and the fellowship which can sustain some dignity. As Jimby's priest said, "When I hear someone speak of 'those damned kids,' I want to know who damned them; that is, who failed to reconcile them after punishment?"

Sir Walter Moberly points out that moral evil, in Christian terms, "cannot be expressed in terms of purely individual responsibility" for "all of us are miserable offenders": judges, bishops, professors, and parents too. Law breaking involves broken relationships with persons and society, and law abiding is not possible without the establishment "of new and richer relationships." He speaks of "the new and unique force, both revolutionary and unexpected" which "bursts the bonds of retributive justice . . . and individual responsibility." But the transforming of evil into good, the work of reclamation of offenders, he says, is slow, tedious, exhausting, full of rebuffs and disappointments. So those who work for establishing reconciling relationships *must have the support and encouragement of us all.*

Jimby's judge pointed out that the justice system cannot build reconciling relationships with hundreds of thousands of juveniles— at present a million a year are arrested. This task of "completing the punishment" can be accomplished only by neighbors, friends, relatives, caring volunteers, those who can love and comfort the youngster before, during, and after the ordeal of punishment. As Jimby's judge said, "Many criminologists are concluding that prisons cannot rehabilitate." Police, courts, and jails can punish, but perhaps someone else must assume responsibility for the rehabilitation and reconciliation which is afterwards essential if the court's objectives are to be accomplished. "Instead of blaming the justice system for failing to prevent crime by punishment," the judge said, "perhaps churches and community agencies should be blamed for their failure to heal and reconcile afterwards." Or as one nurse said, who frequently works with physically-abused youngsters: "Hugging them and loving them is most important."

Punishment is a process by which society now deliberately wounds many youngsters. But how can "hugging" be provided for a fourteen-year-old murderer, a fifteen-year-old arsonist, a fifteen-year-old car thief, pimp, or burglar? Our preface warned against being unrealistic, sentimental, and about generalizations. *There are, however, concrete acts of reconciliation* which you and I can experiment with such as *listening, helping provide support networks, jobs, and supervision* (as suggested in the next chapters).

Punishment, at school or in court, has its ritualistic and symbolic elements since the justice system traditionally uses dramatic symbols to influence the offender and public. Perhaps we should also experiment with symbolic forms of reconciliation—such as a religious service to celebrate the "paying of debt to society"; or another dramatic appearance in court for the award or restoration of withdrawn privileges, followed by a family celebration of forgiveness and the new start. In March, 1977, TV cameras went into the classroom of a teacher who had been nominated for a Jefferson Award to record some of the rituals she used in class to effect reconciliation between her primary pupils and herself. She said that since children do not automatically come to value others, or grow in self-respect, she found it necessary to plan small rituals—similar to the "passing of the peace" in some religious services. Primitive tribes, she said, have rituals to teach children about their rights and duties as well as to restore an offender to status in the tribe. She found that children especially need such rituals after punishment so that without embarrassment they can be reincorporated into the classroom community. Rituals which demonstrate support and thus show that the group values them. The teacher lamented the fact that children who improve their behavior are so rarely complimented and praised for it; and that after punishment they rarely experience any public expression of acceptance and forgiveness.

Churches, schools, camps, and neighborhood organizations do not need to wait for the reform of the justice system to experiment with symbolic reconciliation or to hug and help heal the wounds of youngsters after punishment by the courts.

How Are We Punishing?

Scientific and humane methods to accomplish behavior change are slowly being introduced in families and schools to replace medieval methods which really do not punish at all. It is now against the law to spank any child in Sweden. "The problem is that the penal system and much other school and court punishment," says Dr. Richard Otto, "violates all the principles of effective punishment." Parents and teachers can be helped to define each specific change in behavior which is needed and then use *only* that punishment—or other more effective means—which can effect the precise change which is required. In the next century, as corrections become more scientific, people may laugh at us for referring to executions, for example, as "capital *punishment*." For how did a hanging help the offender to change and grow in character? Citizens of the next century will be as shocked by our prisons and abuses of offenders as we are by slavery.

It is ironic that so many editorial writers, legislators, and other citizens who advocate harsher punishment of juveniles to deter crime really do not know how punishment might really have a significant impact. Even though they live in a scientific age, they view the justice system in ways as medieval as the health-care system would be viewed if physicians still tried to cure patients by draining off their blood. The kinds of harsher punishments now being advocated are calculated deliberately to wound and hurt juveniles—in a sort of "whipping-boy* style" which punishes one child in the hope of changing the behavior of others! The

*A "whipping boy" was another youngster who was whipped whenever a young prince misbehaved.

justice system tries to cure youngsters of crime by draining off their strength and health as we have seen in our seven cases. Even in an age of great scientific advance and imagination, *this medieval philosophy* of "retaliation," to get even with the offender, or of "retribution," to make the criminal pay, *seems to prevent the type of research which might really transform corrections.* The medical research which moved the health-care system out of the Middle Ages dissected every failure and mistake and carefully examined every successful cure. Where is the case-by-case examination of punishments, so that those which fail can be abandoned and replaced?

Defenders of court-style punishment can point out that there are times when we must deliberately wound our children: cutting out tonsils or the appendix, cutting open a snakebite, taking out a splinter,—but afterwards we then give careful attention to healing the wounds.

In the cases of our seven juveniles where is that healing? In some cases it seems as if "official punishments" deliberately seek to keep the wounds open to fester, to prolong the suffering until it becomes torture rather than a punishment designed to accomplish specific changes. And laws are now being debated and passed to increase and intensify this deliberate wounding of youngsters. Yet, punishment can and does reduce crime if scientifically applied. The evidence is conclusive, for example, that fewer people drive the highways at criminal speeds if those who do are promptly arrested and punished; but the rules have to be applied fairly to all. Effective punishment must be prompt and fair, and the driver who loses his license must know how his behavior must change and what he must do to get the license back. If punishment is the application of a stimulus to change specific behavior, we begin to see how to put together the puzzle which these seven stories presented to us. For the most part these juveniles were not really punished at all. They were beaten, imprisoned, suspended from school; over and over, they were wounded in ways that made no sense at all to them or to those who interpreted the meaning of the experience to them.

One clue: R.J. Corsini in *The Practical Parent* (New York: Harper and Row, 1975) shows how people use irrational punishments because of ignorance of what better to do. Such punishments ". . . create resentments . . . character defects, cause youngsters to lose respect for order and to try to get even, and may actually encourage misbehavior." John E. Valusek in *People Are Not for Hitting and Children Are People* (3629 Mossman, Wichita, KS 67200) documents how children learn violence not from TV or the media but at mother's knee and from father's strap.

Specific help for parents, see: Selma Fraiberg, *The Magic Years* (New York: Charles Scribner's Sons, 1959), on the "education of conscience" and the "psychology of punishment." But the real laboratory for experimentation is the everyday experience of parents and teachers with punishment.

Groups in communities and churches can begin to keep a record of all such punishments so as to document which succeed in changing behavior and which fail.

CHAPTER 10

Punishment-One
and
Punishment-Two

IS THERE ANOTHER TYPE of sentencing and punishment which itself might begin the process of changed behavior, growth, reconciliation, and real rehabilitation? Sensitive court officials struggle with that question all the time, but rarely in a context which looks at the total experience of the child with punishment. By the time a juvenile comes to court he has been punished many times at home and at school and the failure of those punishments reflects a lack of consistency and cooperation in his neighborhood. If the justice system's style of punishment, its philosophy, its interpretation to the offender by family, court, and friends are crucial to behavior change and post-punishment reconciliation, then the same is true of a youngster's first experiences with punishment.

Parents, teachers, and others who ought to experiment jointly with a commonly developed philosophy of punishment which can be consistently applied in neighborhoods, need two different words for punishment as suggested by Jimby's judge: "We need to speak of *punishment-one* and *punishment-two* in order to clarify the choices before this court."

Punishment-one: Some see the purpose of punishment as retaliation, retribution, revenge, getting even, striking back in the war against crime. "One cannot sit in court every day," the judge

said, "without realizing that there is a war between the generations in many families and neighborhoods, and another war between the 'system' and those on welfare or who see themselves
as outsiders, permanently unemployed. *Punishment-one* seeks to
arm society to wage these wars more effectively."

Punishment-two, on the other hand, seeks to end such war and
sees as its purpose changed behavior. For example, a specific
goal might be to get a youngster to quit stealing. Jail won't help.
In jail he learns new robbery techniques and practices them by
stealing from other inmates. "Let's be specific and talk about
Jimby," the judge suggested, "and how to apply *punishment-two*
in order to make sure he quits stealing. As in medicine or education,
every offender is different and must be properly diagnosed for
effective treatment; but I think I proceed scientifically—even
though I'm not yet ready to say so publicly—when on the basis
of a case-study approach I have success *with a three-formula
punishment: intensive supervision, confrontation with victims, and
restitution.*"

Jimby's judge has been severely criticized for giving the boy a
suspended sentence, so I asked her to explain how *punishment-
two* might be more effective.

"My goal with Jimby must not be negative; it is not a question
of merely getting him to give up theft. He might then simply
turn to other crimes. I wish I could transform his life through a
series of experiences in cooperation with community agencies,
churches, unions, clubs; but the court's possibilities and alternatives are very limited, unless people and organizations in the
community step forward with offers of help. So instead of jail—
which might turn a smart boy like Jimby into a master criminal—
more creative punishment might be possible. I took extra time
with Jimby because his priest was willing to organize such neighborhood involvement. He and I hope that we can provide a demon-
stration model of what neighbors and organizations can do, which
may ultimately be applicable to many adult criminals also—
especially first offenders."

"So you want to make rehabilitation a community responsibility?"

"And punishment too! *How can punishment deter any other
youngster unless it happens in the neighborhood where he can see
it and really be influenced by it?* Furthermore, as I looked at

Jimby's life-long experience with punishment I saw that preventing his serious crimes—from age eight or so—would have required a more consistent and agreed-upon view and style of punishment in his neighborhood. His well-intentioned mother, simply ignorant of what to do, would have willingly listened to her priest and other parents if they were working together with police, teachers, and court to experiment with a common philosophy of punishment."

"Isn't that rather complicated for neighborhoods like Jimby's, for people without education like Jimby's mother?"

"No, I'm talking about something quite simple, human, perhaps almost instinctive to parents, who would really rather love and care for their children than hit them. *Punishment-two* is the application of a deliberately-selected stimulus to change specific behavior. For example, a mother says to her three-year-old, 'If you run into the street in front of cars I'm going to spank you.' His behavior changes if she does. On the other hand if she says, 'I'm going to spank you unless you are good,' he may puzzle over what that means and there is less likely to be a behavior change. Indeed, he is likely in that case of confused threat to become sullen and ready to hit back when spanked. *But notice that if she really wants to prevent her infant from running into the street, her most effective method of punishment is constant supervision.* She has to watch that small child all the time until he is old and mature enough to be trustworthy and responsible.

"Here we see the foundation for a new style of punishment that can be consistently applied in neighborhoods, schools, families and courts . . . instead of our medieval corporal punishments, capital punishments, and prisons."

"But don't some people have to be locked up for the safety of the community?" I asked.

"If so, then they must be locked up forever and never be released," she said, "because while in prison they are likely to develop such bitterness, hate, and resentments that they will do even greater harm to society once they get out. No, what such people really need if society is to be protected—and penitentiaries were an experiment at providing it on a mass basis—is constant, twenty-four-hour-a-day supervision. And supervision is much more than surveillance. I'll come back to that later. I was just reading a review of the psychiatric research at St. Elizabeth's

Hospital in Washington D.C. by Samenow and Yochelson. On the basis of their fifteen-year intensive study of some 250 hard-core criminals, they have come to agree with J.Q. Wilson of Harvard and others that 'evil people exist,' that some offenders simply can't be rehabilitated. Perhaps because of genetic defects some youngsters very early tend to become 'loners' or seek out other criminals as partners, often feeling that they have a right to steal and kill other people. These researchers believe that it may be possible, in some cases, to 'tear down the criminal personality' and entirely rebuild the character of such people—but it is a long and costly process and can't take place in prison. Such people, Yochelson and Samenow contend, can't be deterred by threat of punishment because they are convinced that they will never be caught . . . or caught again."

"Some criminologists therefore now suggest that prisons give up any pretense at rehabilitation and simply punish," the judge said. "Suppose I am convinced that Jimby is one of those persons who is born with genetic structures that make him a life-long criminal. That's not his fault! Is he to be punished all the rest of his life in jail for the way he was born? No, Samenow and Yochelson suggest that people who need life-long supervision must be placed in non-punitive environments. If they must be locked up, then place them in humane camps with their families—insofar as the families are willing. But, in fact, supervision can be provided in neighborhoods, just as we are discovering how to provide intensive care at home for the elderly, the mentally ill or retarded, and handicapped."

"In any case," I said, "you are working with juveniles."

"And are we to attempt no rehabilitation with a million arrested children? *Punishment-one*, which seeks to scare youngsters so they won't commit crimes, simply isn't working. *Punishment-two*, on the other hand, can eliminate juvenile crime. I'm not joking! There need be no serious juvenile crime if we supervise *all* children intensely, twenty-four hours a day, seven days a week."

Intensive Supervision: Effective Punishment

"If a youngster is arrested, you would treat him as a two-year-old again," I said.

"Precisely! Intensive supervision can be a very painful and effective punishment. For example, I propose a philosophy of supervision such as that developed by the Y.W.C.A.—to supervise staff and program so that everyone involved can be helped to grow, to change, to succeed, so that all can learn from each other. This is quite different from the 'surveillance' philosophy of many prison guards. The staff at our state juvenile training school will go on strike if you suggest that they, too, are supposed to grow and change along with the inmates, even learn from them too. Yet, what I propose is not so different from the philosophy of training schools, which contends that supervision can gradually be relaxed as an offender grows in maturity and self-control; but what the offender really learns there is how to adjust to the institution, not how to be honest on the street. Let me return to my illustration. The young mother who wants to keep her two-year-old out of the street has to supervise him all the time. As he matures she can begin to relax her supervision and let him accept more responsibility for his own behavior and even let him learn from some rather painful mistakes."

"That's where I think interpretation of experiences is crucial."

She nodded. "Yes, good supervision includes planning positive experiences for the youngster—not merely spanking him for mischief when he has nothing constructive to do and it must include interpretation of the meaning of his experiences. Now, I am angry that the newspaper says that I let Jimby off without punishment. I have applied *punishment-two* by insisting on seven-days-a-week supervision for Jimby. It can be very punitive for an adolescent, to be treated again like a two-year-old. The juvenile probation officer doesn't have time to supervise him intensely so I need the help of volunteers, his family, and friends. I especially count on Francine, his wife-to-be. If they fail to provide continuous, constructive supervision, then the punishment fails."

"What is success?"

"No more crime, no more law breaking. It's as simple as that, and preventing juvenile crime must begin at a very early age. First, all youngsters must know clearly what the rules are. After a small child's first offense, supervision is increased. The first time Jimby was arrested, when he was in primary school, he should have been sentenced to attend after-school and evening-supervised activities until he showed himself ready to resume responsibility and self-control. The second time he was arrested, his supervision could have been expanded to weekends. Jails are so expensive that, if necessary, a professional could be employed to supervise him for a time on a one-to-one basis and still save money for the taxpayer. The state of Pennsylvania, for example, is experimenting successfully with intensive supervision by young probation officers, or a college student could be employed to be his roommate and weekend companion for a time. Jimby could, if necessary, be required to carry a two-way radio to keep in constant communication with his supervisor."

"I understand there are serious experiments with electronic supervision, a monitoring device which an offender might be required to carry so that his probation officer knows at all times where he is."

She shook her head. "Delinquency is usually a symptom of a youngster's need for more personal attention, for more meaningful relationships with people. I don't think kids can be kept from crime by surveillance, no matter how many cops and corridor guards you employ . . . or by machines. *Youngsters are kept from crime only by people who demonstrate real caring.* I could suspend Jimby's sentence because he has a family and friends who care, and brothers who are notorious for keeping their word. Jimby's real salvation, of course, is his baby. He's crazy about that child. It is no coincidence that a majority of youngsters drop out of crime and delinquency when they establish such relationships."

"You recommend closer supervision as school punishment too?"

"I'm angry at schools that 'punish' by suspending or expelling pupils to roam the streets unsupervised. Some schools are now punishing, instead, with 'in-school suspension' that takes a disruptive child out of the classroom—so that others can study—and places him or her in a closely supervised room for one-to-one counseling and tutoring. It would be cheaper by far to employ a second and third set of teachers to extend the school day to keep youngsters in supervised activities until suppertime and evenings than to jail a youngster at a cost of $20,000 or more a year. A second effective punishment, used mostly by parents, is taking away privileges until more responsible behavior is demonstrated; but so many of the youngsters who come to this court have few privileges. Their lives are so empty and impoverished that positive supervision must be imposed to fill their lives with interesting, educational things they enjoy doing. What is needed is not for volunteers to give *more* time so much as a redirection of the time they have to give. Neighborhood activities and organizations can be used *within the structure of a well-thought-out philosophy of punishment.*"

She pointed to a wall chart which she and Jimby's priest had prepared to propose a coordination and mobilization of neighborhood resources. "They say that Jimby's neighborhood lacks services —but look at all the possibilities we found! A plan could easily have been developed and implemented for closer supervision of Jimby and his brothers from a very early age. Even the police there were very fond of Jimby. It is ironic that this affection was not communicated to the boy in terms of *caring help*. All the resources were present. All that was needed was for a few people to give some time and thought to planning and coordination. Jimby's priest has found some women in the parish who are going to show what can be done for one kid and family by a network of caring friends, by a shift of emphasis in some programs, by some training of persons in supervision."

"What should the role of neighborhood police be?" I asked.

The judge replied angrily. "Do their job! I recently complimented one young officer who has reduced offenses to almost zero in a high-crime neighborhood when he is on duty. Where other officers conduct surveillance from police cars, he gets out of his car as much as possible to cultivate a personal acquaintance with people in every block. In addition to working with neighborhood organizations he seeks out people whose work or residence location gives them a commanding view of the street. These people can be supervisors! Elderly people who sit at their windows often see suspicious behavior, but in Jimby's neighborhood they rarely report such things to the police because they are afraid. They do not know one police officer they can trust in a situation where they might face retaliation. This young officer began to win the trust of such people by reassuring them of his personal help, by being present at a promised time when they need to go to the bank or store. Crime greatly decreased in his area because he secured the active help of cooperating volunteers. In Germany such 'contact police', specially trained in supervision, have been very effective in reducing crime."

Confrontation with Victims

"Where the court and schools really need the cooperation of citizens is in a second phase of *punishment-two*: the changing of a youngster's behavior by confronting him or her with the consequences of crime. I've puzzled a lot," the judge said, "about how to get people to care: teachers, nurses, social workers, kids like Jimby. Why did some people risk their lives to hide Jewish children from the Nazis where others did not? Philip Hallie in *Lest Innocent Blood Be Shed* (New York: Harper and Row, 1979) tells how even Nazi officials and soldiers were sometimes transformed —and secretly helped those who were hiding Jewish children— when they encountered people with the strength to care. Because 'caring was infectious.' One person helping a kid can inspire others to do so. But it is awfully hard to get victims to care."

"Jimby's victim refused to sit down for a talk with you and him."

She frowned. "No. I had in mind something like the incident reported in *Corrections* magazine, January, 1975. A clergyman and his wife were asked to sit down with the burglar who had robbed their home and they found it difficult to do that. Going to jail to see him was painful for them, but it was important because it was even more painful for the burglar—in the best sense of transforming punishment. The burglar later said that the encounter made him feel "awful cheap and low because they were such nice people." His redemption from crime was accelerated— not by a sentimental experience—but through a personal relationship established with his victims. He worked out with them a plan to pay them back for what he had stolen. He feels good about that, and this sense of self-worth, more than anything else, is what these youngsters need."

I thought of Emilio, whose life could have been salvaged perhaps if he could have gone to see the woman he hurt, if he could have been helped to attempt some compensation to her. But the experience of a Black foster father, in handling a serious crime by one of his children, perhaps best illustrates how *punishment-two* can be creative, redemptive, and reconciling. The foster son came from an environment where he had been taught that—while stealing might be wrong—it was quite proper to keep stolen goods because "possession is nine-tenths of the law." The youngster was angry when his foster father insisted that he return a stolen cassette tape recorder. And the store manager at first refused to talk to the thief. He had no interest in 'wasting his time on a little bum who had been in and out of court.' The father insisted, however, and had already cultivated police support for the act of restitution and apology. So the store manager finally did give an evening to talking it out with the boy.

"To listening as well as lecturing?" Jimby's judge asked as I told the story.

"Yes, the young thief volunteered to contribute some free labor in exchange for the manager's trouble, but a thief wasn't wanted around the store—to learn about the burglar alarms and so forth. With offers of police supervision, the boy did go to work at the shop. As a result he became interested in having a store of his own sometime. He became sympathetic with the manager's problems with shoplifting and helped develop some plans to reduce such theft. In time the store manager became the youngster's friend and the boy became a trusted, valued employee. His behavior changed to such an extent that he became a strong anti-crime influence in his previously criminal gang and he and his friends became really effective agents of crime prevention in the neighborhood."

"With *punishment-one* this could never have been accomplished," the judge said. "But to arrange more of this sort of confrontation with victims the court must have much more help and cooperation from everyone in the neighborhood and especially from victims!"

Restitution as Effective Punishment

Theoretically a juvenile who breaks a window should pay for replacing it; or even better, he should be involved in the physical work of replacing the broken glass himself. But society must be realistic about the amount of time that most people are willing to give to restitution, however good it may be for the offender. Juvenile probation officers do not have the time and most youngsters don't have the skill to replace a window without supervision. "So," I said, "The court uses *punishment-one* because people in the community don't offer enough help to make more creative punishments work?"

Jimby's judge nodded. "I had what you might call a 'screaming encounter' at a labor union meeting recently. I was invited to talk about preventing juvenile crime and the union members hated everything I had to say. They wanted me to talk about ways to 'get even' with kids or adults who steal their cars or mug their grandmothers. They wanted to talk about long prison sentences for delinquent kids—except their own. I told them that *any working person who is concerned about crime prevention ought to volunteer to work with offenders on restitution.* I told them that if every concerned worker in the country would spend a bit of time each week helping one delinquent learn a job skill by undertaking some constructive restitution—we could turn the misdirected justice system around and work a miracle of crime prevention. But the members of that union didn't want to hear me say that the kid who broke a window needs some man to work alongside him in repairing it. No, it was against union rules, one man said angrily. Anyway, it was too much trouble. They want to employ police to prevent crime—as they want to employ physicians to keep them from having heart attacks caused by their overeating and overdrinking."

"But you can't blame the average citizen . . ."

"We are all victims of a system that has become too depersonalized and only the involvement of average citizens can repersonalize it. In theory, the boy who puts out a man's eye in a criminal attack helps pay the man's medical bills and helps support the blinded man's family through taxes and insurance. Instead of meeting the blinded man, to have the chance to eat supper with him and his family, the criminal is told that he has committed an offense *against the state* and must 'pay his debt' to society, not to the victim. Many youngsters today see the state as the enemy, as the oppressor who gives them bad schools, bad housing, no jobs. They couldn't care less about the state. So I sentenced Jimby to work four nights a week—for a full year at least—in a hospital emergency room, where he can help people suffering from auto accidents like the one he caused. Usually the court doesn't really have the time and opportunity to get well enough acquainted with an offender to discover what kind of restitution could really change future behavior. I advocate—in every punishment from a very young age—the drawing up of a contract between punisher and offender with outside supervisors involved to guarantee the fairness and completion of the contract."

She picked up Jimby's contract from her desk. "Jimby has a Catholic feeling for penance so I felt that each time he helps some hurt person in the emergency room he can feel that he is undertaking some restitution for the hurt he caused. When I draw up a contract it must include:

—a statement of the precise offense which society is required to punish

—a statement of the required behavior change which is expected

—a statement of the privileges withdrawn and the intensive supervision imposed as punishment

—a step-by-step delineation of specific acts of restitution, job training, or whatever that must be completed before the privileges are restored and the intensive supervision relaxed

—there is a time frame and procedure for termination and revising the contract, with special recognition when the terms are fulfilled

—and most important, the contract makes clear who is responsible for working with the offender to provide the guidance, help, and support to make it possible for him to succeed in carrying out the terms of the contract—especially skill development, life enrichment, and constructive supervision.

Group and Network Support

"So you see," the judge concluded, "*punishment-two* requires what I call 'group sentencing,' a term which must not be confused with the efforts of some courts to punish parents for the offenses of their children. I can't expect Jimby to succeed on his own, without the help of citizens in his neighborhood. Supervision, restitution, dialogue with victims, nearly all of the elements of *punishment-two* require the participation of a network of people."

"But how can the court punish innocent people who had no part in the crime?"

"I'm concerned about implementing a process to change be-

havior and that involves punishment in a context of love. Courts
and jails can't be loving nor can the isolated juvenile. Changed
behavior requires a development of conscience, making use of
feelings of guilt, of a youngster's wish to belong, and that isn't
possible in isolation. A juvenile's behavior can be changed through
a process of growth into maturity and responsibility, a good life
only insofar as he or she is helped to establish warm, supportive,
reconciling human relationships. And that is the job of people
in the neighborhood, not of the courts and police."
Where can you begin? George Washnis in *Citizen Involvement in
Crime Prevention* (Lexington, Mass.: Lexington Books, 1976) proposes block associations and other neighborhood organizations
working in cooperation with the police . . . including "junior
patrols." He says, "It often takes youth to deal effectively with
youth," and "police performance is largely influenced by the de-
gree citizens see themselves concerned and insistent on quality
service."

Seattle Accountability Boards (313½ First Avenue, Seattle,
Wash., 98104) sets up panels of five or six persons from the
community to help a youngster make restitution in cases of theft
and vandalism to make him aware "that he is responsible for
his behavior towards himself and the community." Judge Albert
Kramer of East Norfolk District Court, Quincy, Mass., has developed an extensive restitution program which places offenders
in hospitals and nursing homes, many choosing to remain permanently in such service jobs after their "debt is paid." *In
areas where 90 per cent of offenders return to crime after imprisonment, the return rate after these restitution programs is as low
as 7 per cent.* San Francisco's Legal Services for Children Clinic,
for example, helped place a twelve-year-old mugger of the elderly
in a part-time job at a senior citizen's center where he could get
acquainted personally with the kind of people he had been mugging.

Volunteer-in-Probation (200 Washington Square Plaza, Royal
Oak, Mich., 58067) grows out of Judge Keith Leenhouts' pioneer-
ing work to change the lives of young criminals through creative
supervision.

In our neighborhoods, while we wait for long-range solutions,
we can all get involved in five types of "water boiling" and

"sandbagging" as suggested in the next chapters. First Congregational Church, Stamford, Conn., for example, attempts to reconcile offenders who return to the community, with vocational and therapeutic guidance, housing, education, and employment. Of the 250 persons this church has helped, only three have returned to jail. A remarkable success record.

CHAPTER 11

Listening

RECONCILIATION begins with listening. It is difficult for an offender to be restored to a human place in society, to be reconciled after punishment, if he feels he has not had a fair hearing. Yet an article on "Monitoring the Juvenile Justice System" (*American Criminal Law Review*, September, 1974) reports that when a hundred juveniles are arrested in an urban crime area only twenty of them will get a hearing and only forty will even go to court.

Bertie's criminalization is closely related to the rage that still burns in him over not being allowed to tell his side of the story in court, or before being suspended from school. His reconciliation with society requires some way for him to let his feelings and emotions pour out—in a way that no doubt would require more time than the court could give and, as his lawyer put it, "far beyond the necessity of the court." Yet if our legal system must require a defendent to keep silent in many cases—so as not to testify against himself—then other means must be found for a youngster like Bertie to say what he needs to say. Even his mother did not listen to his side of the case in a way that satisfied him, nor did his busy young court-appointed lawyer. In any case, Bertie did not feel a need to confess to his mother, lawyer, or priest, although that might have made a contribution to his reconciliation. He wanted to tell his story to the teacher and principal who unfairly suspended him, and to the father of the boy he stabbed, and to a jury of his peers that would give him a fair hearing; then he would have been prepared to "pay his debt" for what he really did, accepting as fair any punishment meted out by those who really knew the truth about what happened.

John Holt speaks of a boy like Bertie who sat in a court room where several adults were discussing his case. The fifteen-year-old kept muttering, "All I want is a fair trial like anyone else." Holt says, "He might as well have saved his breath. He wasn't going to get a fair trial or any trial." Psychologists and court officials were going to decide what to do with his life without reference to his own wishes and *without adequate consultation with him* about what he would consider fair and helpful. Bertie feels that the schools always did this too.

But if people in Bertie's neighborhood begin to experiment with hearings to correct such feelings, the place to begin is with very young children. One of Bertie's teachers said, "Kids at our school have hardly ever in their lives had a hearing before punishment. First at home, then at school, finally in court these boys feel that their pride and manhood is somehow manipulated away as they are slapped down again and again without a satisfying chance to be heard. In fact, trying to 'talk back' to the teacher or parent is an excuse for being slapped down again." Bertie would not have been in the emotional state which facilitated the unnecessary stabbing if, before his suspension, the school had given him a hearing to tell about his problems. As a victim of extortioners, he also needed a hearing to get justice at a much earlier age. We often forget that youngsters are often victims of crime before they become offenders.

Some states are now reducing to thirteen the age at which a juvenile can be tried as an adult for serious crimes, but isn't thirteen entirely too late? Jimby and Hector were involved in serious thefts at the age of seven and eight. Society does not delay drastic measures when a youngster shows symptoms of serious illness. Theft or other early childhood offenses could be the occasion for neighborhood or school hearings to deal promptly with the situation before the youngster slips gradually into more serious offenses. Methods for involving very young children in responsible trials and hearings are demonstrated by the Bemposta Circus School. Children there accept responsibility for disciplining each other and do not for a moment put up with classroom disruption. Any child feeling wronged can ask for a hearing so that whatever caused misbehavior can be sought out and solved.

The youngsters at this "children's republic" in Spain have themselves worked out a procedure for hearings based on the point of view *that every act of misbehavior has underlying causes as a result of mistakes committed by the entire community* and not merely by the offender. Hearings are conducted with solemn pageantry copied from adult courts, but the goal of each hearing is always *to help everyone in the community get insight into how all of them have failed each other and the offender.* Even six-year-olds at Bemposta would immediately have demanded a public hearing if they had the sort of incompetent substitute teacher that couldn't keep order in Bertie's class, much less teach math.

"Justice for pupils is not wanted at our school," one of Bertie's teachers said. "Because school administrators and teachers want to be totalitarian dictators rather than spending time and effort with parents and pupils in real student self-government with hearings and with student-enacted laws. Yet, today, most teachers desperately need help in this area. If we are going to teach successfully we can't spend so much energy on police work in class and halls. Parents and volunteers could help, at least with hearings."

"When are children old enough to make and enforce rules?" I asked. "Or to petition for hearings before punishment?"

"Children are old enough when adults begin scolding them for not acting more responsibly and grown-up. The process of preparing youngsters for self-discipline requires an earlier apprenticeship in the arts of self-control and self-government. Perhaps not in the schools, at least at first, but *there can be experimentation* in churches, camps, families, and youth organizations."

Lena attended a high school which insisted that inner-city youngsters couldn't assume adult responsibility in self-discipline at school; yet her gang demonstrated great effectiveness in organization and self-discipline, and at changing the behavior of any gang member who endangered security.

Neighborhood Juvenile Hearings

Paul Lerman, reporting on the successful use of citizens on boards to deal with juvenile offenders (*Transaction,* July/Aug.,

1971) suggests that when juvenile justice professionals object to the use of ordinary citizens and volunteers, it should be pointed out to them *that the justice system does not yet have a very successful record* in curing or preventing crime and delinquency such as the medical profession might use to justify opposition to the use of volunteers. He points out that ". . . many judges and police are also untrained or inadequately trained for dealing with juveniles." He suggests that volunteers "*can be trained to listen* and may give more time and preparation to juvenile cases than busy professionals." Lerman concludes, "Citizens who share a similar life-style and are knowledgeable about the problems of growing up in a given community may be in a better position to enact a *parens patriae* doctrine than are professionals or judges."

Juveniles are themselves serving as judges and juries for minor offenses of other children in an increasing number of American communities such as Glen Cove, Long Island. (I have not found any adequate study and evaluation of such youth-run courts and hearings.) Since a court of juveniles alone may appear as a game and therefore not be taken seriously by adults and youngsters, an adult-youth partnership in neighborhood hearings could provide youngsters with a forum to which they could appeal for justice.

Even in advance of legislative authorization, neighborhood organizations can experiment with variations of a proposal made by the Deans of Antioch Law School for "neighborhood courts" —at least experimentation can be undertaken with minor pre-arrest offenses of younger children. The Antioch Deans suggest that court hearings be held in the youngster's neighborhood, in the evening or at a time when family and concerned friends could easily be present. The involvement of friends and relatives is needed to provide the effective supervision required for success in behavior change. The Antioch Deans also feel that the court could better understand the offender and his offense by visiting his street and home.

"But," as one of Bertie's teachers said, "society seems only interested in retaliation *after* a killing instead of the simple, humane things that could have prevented the schoolyard murder in the first place."

A report in the *American Criminal Law Review,* Sept. 1974, tells of innovative efforts in Scotland to enlist the cooperation of youngsters themselves in hearings for children which are conducted by panels of volunteers. *Neighborhood Justice Centers,* an October 1977 publication of the United States Justice Department, discusses "informal settings" for the mediation and conciliation of neighborhood disputes, landlord-tenant arguments, and some juvenile cases —a model somewhat like the "tribal moots" in Liberia. S.C. Kahn ("It's Time to Teach Jurisprudence in High School," *Social Studies,* January, 1975) points the way to helping inner-city and other youngsters take more interest in school by studying law, crime, justice, and courts in relation to their own offenses and victimization.

The Vera Institute of Justice report to the Ford Foundation on violent delinquents found that there can be no significant prevention of juvenile crime without *enlisting the active cooperation of juveniles* themselves and their families.

Today a majority of American young persons are breaking laws regularly. Not only drug laws, speed laws, sex laws; one study found 56 per cent of fourteen-to-eighteen-year-olds in Illinois reported either keeping or using stolen goods at one time or another; 60 per cent of pupils polled in a hundred average high schools said that their rights were regularly being violated by school officials without their having any right to appeal. They said they were regularly subjected to arbitrary, undemocratic, and unfair acts and decisions without fair hearings. On the other hand, the *New York Times,* May 27, 1979, reported that teen-age juries in New Mexico and Illinois had helped reduce delinquency by as much as 50 per cent.

Volunteers in Juvenile Justice (published by the L.E.A.A., U.S. Department of Justice, October, 1977) suggests how volunteers can be recruited, trained, supervised, and used to help provide alternatives for juveniles in court. The section on "The Church as Volunteer in Courts and Corrections" points out "that change in the criminal justice system is long overdue" and "it is time for churches to speak and act." Not only can churches and neighborhood organizations experiment with hearings, they can monitor existing hearings and can provide recognition and praise for volunteers and professionals who deserve it. The *Model Volunteer*

Project (California Volunteer Programs in Corrections, 222 Sierra Blvd., Sacramento, Cal., 95825) reports that only about half of the agencies using volunteers provide adequate recognition and appreciation. Almost anyone could help with this.

The National Council of Juvenile Court Judges (Box 800, Reno, Nev., 89507) publishes a *Handbook for Volunteers in Juvenile Court* which suggests reconciling acts of volunteers with young offenders such as "providing a child in trouble with meaningful one-to-one relationships with an adult he can trust"; tutoring, counseling, court-watching, leadership for group sessions with parents and offenders; job hunting, life enriching, giving attention and affection, providing transportation, *and listening.*

Have you done what you can to support Big Brothers/Big Sisters in your community?

CHAPTER 12

Detention in Good Company

WISHER'S CRIMINAL CAREER and jail suicide before his fourteenth birthday could have been prevented, if the state had better places for the detention of runaways and offenders, if he could have been placed in "good company" rather than with youngsters who harmed each other with violent assaults, rapes, and beatings with chains. State councils of churches and the League of Women Voters have been searching for alternatives which can also begin the process of reconciliation.

One is the "host home" program which recruits families to receive runaway youngsters as temporary guests to keep them out of jails. California, in some cases, now uses "house arrest"—requiring arrested youngsters to stay at home under continuous supervision until trial. A goal of such alternatives is suggested by Judge David Bazelton who asked the League of Women Voters, "How do we treat children we really care about? We feed them, comfort them, play with them, swat them once in a while, and *most of all warm them with our love and pride*. We don't as a rule isolate them for weeks as punishment for minor offenses, or make them account for every five minutes of their time, or deny them privacy, or refuse them all contact with the opposite sex"—as happens when they are "detained for their own protection." Bertie was well treated in jail, but he was befriended by inmates who told him that he would never again be able to escape the stigma of being a jailbird and murderer just as he could never escape the stigma of being Black in a white society. They taught him how to become hard, tough, to fight with a razor blade, how to survive on the street through crime. When he came home he told his mother, "A suspended sentence, Mom, is a reputation they give you so you can't ever again be like other people or get a decent job."

If some young people have to be institutionalized for their own safety, or for that of the community, then religious people must respond with the sort of creative energy which in earlier generations led them to establish schools, hospitals, summer camps, and other innovations. Heinz Vonhoff in *People Who Care* (Philadelphia: Fortress Press, 1960) speaks of the community of Bethel-über-Bielefeld in West Germany which established a uniquely successful reformatory alongside institutions for epileptics, the mentally retarded, the elderly, a theological and music school, and so forth. Bethel succeeded in transforming young criminals with means *so simple as to seem common sense*. Instead of incarcerating the delinquents with other criminals, they spent all their time in association with people who were devoting their lives to helping epileptics or in hospitals, working alongside a chaplain, a nurse, a social worker, a student, or a physician. They read to the elderly, played with sick children, and began to develop purposeful ideas for school and future work. The juvenile left Bethel without the onus of a jail reputation or reformatory record, but with a praiseworthy social-work experience. And this transformation was accomplished without the expensive trappings of usual incarceration.

Volunteers can help create a mood in America for expanding such programs here, as indicated by Tom Wicker's report on a crime and prison reform conference at a church in Florida (*New York Times,* Feb. 16, 1979), where he was encouraged to discover "a steady undercurrent of humanity and common sense" . . . still flowing in this "crime-frightened country." The Vera Institute of Justice, after research into alternatives, recommended Outward Bound to help youngsters come to terms with themselves and to help them develop meaningful relationships through a program of wilderness survival. Less publicized is a similar correctional program in Florida which pits youngsters against the sea to give them skills and self-confidence, as well as providing camaraderie and wholesome associations in the midst of the challenge to physical survival. The report on this program in *Corrections,* Sept. 1974, said, "We teach kids that if they do good things, good things can happen to them, too."

Institutions Can Be Creative

A Spanish priest, Father Jesus Silva Mendez, saw the film *Boy's Town* which suggested to him the idea of helping juveniles transform their lives through a children's republic centered around a circus school. The priest had grown up in a circus family and knew its lure to runaways, as well as its challenge to personal achievement. He began the Bemposta community in 1956, seeking to create a community of children which must never be completed—so that each new arrival could be challenged to play his or her part in the development of its philosophy, programs, and institutions. Bemposta is rooted in an understanding of Christianity as struggle—of human society to solve its problems and create itself and of each youngster to create his own life. Eberhard Mobius in *The Children's Republic* (New York: Avon, 1973) reported that the actual heart of the community is the monastery of San Pedro de Rocas from which radiate the currents of strength which inspire the youngsters.

The children at Bemposta dream of infusing the whole world with a new spirit, as recognized by the gold peace medal awarded to them by the United Nations. Father Silva began with street boys who otherwise might have been stealing in Barcelona or Madrid and gave each of them a vision which he might bring into reality in his own life through hard persevering work. "Where else," a New York reporter asked, "can you see eight-year-old aerialists dance on a high wire to a rock beat?" The youngsters must learn to sing, dance, play musical instruments, and master all the skills of highly professional circus performers. "There's no place like our community," one long-haired young acrobat told the reporter. "We have a truly democratic society, a city of children where we run everything: shops, bakery, factory, and the school, which teaches hotel management, catering, carpentry, and other skills."

The journalist asked Father Silva about discipline problems—

when hundreds of youngsters go on the road for performances each night and are taught each day in the tent—and the priest replied, "We have very little misbehavior *because they look after each other*." A new arrival at Bemposta finds that he is self-supporting. The first thing he must do when he arrives is go to the child-run store to arrange credit for a mattress if he is to sleep. He must then get work to pay for his food, his clothing, his very survival. Along with other jobs youngsters at Bemposta are paid for school attendance, because it is seen to be serious work. School is taken seriously by the youngsters because they want to learn to operate their own radio and TV station or to perform in the circus. Schoolwork is also taken seriously because pupils and teachers work together as equals, indeed the youngsters take an active role in selecting and discharging their teachers. In order that spontaneity and creativity will not be crippled the adults are merely advisors in the educational process. Mobius says, "Everything seems to stimulate the children's creativity. Everything in their community gives wing to fantasy and sets no limits to the desire to build, to make, to invent, and to discover."

How does this circus school compare with American training schools or even public schools? Despite the applause and publicity the young circus performers receive, they are invariably found by visitors to be modest, hard-working, self-disciplined, articulate, excelling in their educations. They are excited to feel that they are playing a role in the creation of a better society and this is communicated to the people who attend their circus performances. They dramatize their vision, their message of love and peace for the children of the world, singing, "Lord, give us victory without war: victory over hunger, over money, over vice which destroys the spirit and stifles songs. If all the people of the world will but clasp hands as we do, the spirit of love and peace can govern the world." Can youngsters be trusted to make their own rules? The first rule of Bemposta is, "A citizen loves his fellow citizen like a brother and is always ready to sacrifice for him."

William Glasser in *The Identity Society* (New York: Harper and Row, 1972) proposed experimentation with "community involvement centers" as alternatives to juvenile incarceration. Glasser has been experimenting with schools and communities that wish to replace punishment—which takes responsibility away from youngsters—with positive behavior-reinforcement methods in which teachers "always have a personal relationship with pupils." He says that adults and youngsters must all work together cooperatively in the school to create a "good place" in which courtesy, laughter, communication, and responsibility thrive. A West German program of "pupil representatives" (See *Scala,* Number 4, 1978) has replaced punishment with a system which makes pupils equal partners in resolving problems. They discover that "school problems are really political problems."

Psychologist Fritz Redl (*Parade,* May 1, 1977) warns that society is breeding a generation of hostile youngsters whose "sense of self-worth comes from triumphing over the adult world," from which they feel excluded, through delinquency. The antidote suggested by the Children's Rights Organization (Box 9494, Marina Del Rey, Calif.) is that youngsters under age eighteen be placed on the boards of all agencies dealing with youth—including foster-home agencies, schools, and prisons. If the neighborhood problem with juveniles is serious, then youngsters need even larger involvement in community life at every level. Whether one agrees with that suggestion or not, neighborhood "water boiling" interim solutions must begin by listening to and involving a majority of youngsters themselves.

Note the role of older children in the operation of the school and community of *Nuestros Pequenos Hermanos* in Cuernavaca, Mexico: E. Bernath, *You Are My Brother* (Suite 104, 100 West Camelback Road, Phoenix, Arizona 85013).

CHAPTER 13

Developing Talents

HEALING AND RECONCILIATION after punishment, which is the task of friends, relatives, and volunteers, must involve both life enrichment and development claim the inmates at Walpole prison, who in June, 1974, set out to examine their life experiences to find out why they had been led into crime. Their document, used by the Massachusetts Council of Churches, says: "Listen to us if you want to know what to do about crime which is no more a mystery than other human conduct. Crime is a type of behavior that reveals fundamental flaws in the way society nurtures some children. *Crime results from a failure of development.* A young individual becomes negative when his creative capacities are frustrated. Everything from flowers to trees, to persons and societies, needs to be properly developed and must be cultivated to grow in healthy ways."

A careful investigation into the life and experience of any one criminal, they said, would reveal a frustrated potential: a child who was hurt and criminalized in his struggle to survive and grow. The inmates pleaded with society to listen to the youngsters who struggle against great odds, to understand how their early misbehavior is "acting out" to try *to tell where it hurts.*

The long-range solution may be an entirely new kind of one-to-one tailor-made education based on an individualized assessment of each youngster's unique potential and talents. Meanwhile we can at least recruit people to work with youngsters on one-to-one relationships and we can experiment with "boiling-water" methods of helping them set goals and develop themselves. Since American society has assigned this responsibility to education, the citizens and volunteers who seek *to reconcile through development* will need to work with the schools. Wisher never learned to read. Hector's truck-driver father, oddly enough, never seemed to realize his son's tremendous athletic potential. One of Hector's teachers said, "What was missing from that boy's life was a comprehensive development plan worked out in co-operation with parents, school, church, and others." What would such a plan involve? Hector's pastor, teacher, Sunday School teacher, and a social worker met to answer that question.

One suggestion: a Recognition Book—for family, school, church, scouts, everyone involved—for recording goals and accomplishments. "We take it for granted," a teacher said, "that every child will have a medical record so that important information is not lost but is readily available to teachers, parents, coaches, to other physicians." Hector's pastor said, "I'm distressed to find that the church kept no record of Hector's spiritual growth and experiences, not a single note on his spiritual potential and needs nor on his growth experiences. I imagine that within twenty years we will have a computer record of each youngster, perhaps on the model of Dr. Lawrence Weed's comprehensive computer medical record system in which each patient participates fully in defining his own goals and preferences, in the formulation of plans to solve his problems. Weed found that physicians often fail to keep careful records of problems that need solving, so he prepared a problem-oriented record system which includes economic, social, emotional, as well as physiological data, problems, plans, and progress records."

Another suggestion: an "achievement party" for every youngster on his or her birthday in which the year's accomplishments were publicly noted and praised, including physical goals (how many push-ups now in comparison to last year), cultural goals (what talents are being discovered and developed), citizenship development (community projects and achievements). Hector's pastor said, "I was puzzled by his seeming failure to care about people he blackmailed until I saw him change as he began to receive compliments, affection, and praise for his acrobatic skiing accomplishments. He now seems to care much more for others, since his own accomplishments have given him a greater sense of his own self-worth."

The Bemposta circus community offers each youngster a "year of great adventure," when he or she is fifteen or sixteen. Each young person is challenged to give a year to exploring life at its most difficult points—lest they find life too easy and sheltered in their circus school. They begin the year with a disciplined period of preparation—sleeping on a hard wooden plank, preparing their own meals over an open fire, and maintaining a half-hour of silence twice a day. Their year of service and development actually begins, however, when they go to contribute a month of service as hospital aides; the next month they go to work alongside men who have very hard jobs such as fishermen or they go to a snowbound mountain village.

A fourth month is spent in a juvenile jail as a prisoner to share the lives and hardships of less privileged youngsters. At first the adventurers had to steal a bicycle—for which the sentence was one month, but now Spanish juvenile justice officials cooperate in jailing them so that they remain anonymous and hence are treated no differently than the other inmates. After a month in jail each adventurer contributes a month of work to a social agency in urban slums, the sort of neighborhood from which their fellow jail inmates had come.

After six months of encountering life's most difficult problems in the raw, each adventurer spends a month as a beggar wandering from village to village to learn what it is like to have nothing, to see how society despises and abuses the poor. As in jail they must not let anyone know they are from Bemposta. They must suffer as other beggars, except that they are allowed to travel in groups of two or three so that they can support each other as they experience the degrading loneliness of abject poverty. When these adventurers return to the community, they often enlarge the vision of all the Bemposta youngsters, helping confirm the community's dedication to building strong people committed to change society. The adventurers also experience the year as a search for God "who is found," the returning youngsters report,

"precisely in those places where people suffer and are in need."
Thus the adventure helps them develop new depths of personality,
character, and compassion.

The Rev. Robert Forsberg, reporting on successful church efforts
to improve the quality of public education said, "The churches
know that education should be a lifetime experience and must
take place within a community . . . that the word *educate* comes
from a root, meaning to 'nourish' or 'feed' . . . that the offering
of love through a sharing community is as important to education
as learning theory. William Sanders in *Juvenile Delinquency* (New
York: Praeger, 1976) reports the failure of schools, probation
officers, social agencies, families, and others to coordinate their
efforts. There is no system, he says. Various agencies undercut
each other instead of cooperating in the interests of the child. He
suggests that citizen volunteers can monitor and untangle the
"system" in many communities so that programs can be re-
organized around developmental goals for children. The Children's
Defense Fund (1520 New Hampshire Ave., N.W., Washington, D.C.
20036) prepared a pamphlet entitled, "Your School Records,"
to inform parents and pupils of their right to see and to correct
their records under the Educational Rights and Privacy Act of
1974. Many children receive better treatment merely because some
interested person takes the trouble to ask questions.

CHAPTER 14

Helping Families

"WHAT COULD have been done to prevent Danny's crimes?" I asked his psychiatrist, assuming that he would advocate therapy at an early age for each of these seven youngsters. "Or perhaps I should ask, what role do you see for therapy in the reconciliation process, in the healing and restoring of youngsters to society after their punishment?"

"Not therapy for the youngster alone," he replied. "The entire family needs help. Progress in reducing serious juvenile crime requires more attention to the family as a whole—as the unit of care rather than just the individual."

The evidence from the experience of all our seven juveniles tends to confirm that all families, all people need help at one time or another, and that the individual juvenile delinquent cannot be treated in isolation from his family or his support network of people.

"Where," the psychiatrist asked, "did American society get the idea that a person or family should be ashamed of needing help? Or the feeling that only certain troubled families need guidance and assistance? As with cancer, too many families wait until it is too late to admit the problems they have. All families are troubled at times and in need of outside help."

Support Networks

Many support groups are emerging in communities today, and often in churches, to help bring together people who face similar

143

problems: Alcoholics Anonymous, families whose children have leukemia, parents whose children have died of crib death, women who have breast cancer. Clusters of parents who face similar problems with their adolescents go camping together, taking along some single-parent families and some foster parents and children. "But still most families fail to give thought to their need for deeper relationships with other people, or assume this is rather automatically provided by clubs and churches without much planning and effort on their part," the psychiatrist said.

One model for supporting families is provided by the Downey Side Program in Springfield, Mass., which will be the subject of a sequel book to this volume. Downey Side recruits families to adopt legally the older delinquents who have been thought to be unadoptable. The program succeeds because a network of support is built around the families who make the effort. These adoptive parents meet together to exchange ideas and for mutual support; the community of people who help raise money and help remodel homes for such families, and recruited parents, gathers each Friday night in a remodeled barn for fellowship, worship, and discussion. Downey Side families are helped to succeed with difficult older teenagers because the organization—in ways which could be done by people in almost any community—mobilizes and coordinates a range of services such as a twenty-four-hour-a-day telephone number for emergencies. Downey Side tries first to help the youngster's own family, and if they can't cope, then a second family is recruited for the juvenile with the conviction that more than anything else every youngster needs a caring, competent, responsible, and permanent family.

This is a "stunning idea," some observers feel, and it is one that can be put to work in almost any neighborhood within the framework of existing resources and services. Howard James said in *Children in Trouble:* "It is possible to find children who are being hurt today. Now at this very moment. These children need our help . . . all children need love . . . and the opportunity to reach their highest potential; and not to be held captive in a custodial institution." Interdisciplinary support networks around families have been experimented with by the Middleboro-Lakeville Mental Health Center in Massachusetts, as described in a 1969–71 report: "A step beyond counseling is to bring the client's social network, all the individuals closest to him, into a 'problem solving team.' " This approach makes use of all care givers: clergy, teachers, social workers, police, school counselors, mental health workers. The most effective way to reconcile youngsters after court punishment may in many cases be to enfold their "deficient families" within neighborhood clusters where families reach out to each other and support each other.

The *New London Day*, May 8, 1979, reported a survey on juvenile justice in which Connecticut residents asked for quicker and tougher punishment for youths who repeatedly commit serious crimes; but they insisted at the same time that they want more emphasis on community and family services. Eighty-one per cent agreed that, for example, "when a kid runs away the whole family needs help." Bronfenbrenner suggests that volunteers and community groups could undertake audits to find out what is happening to children who are "coming home to an empty house," expecially one empty of caring.

Danny's pastor said, "When I came to this affluent surburb from the inner city I was surprised to find so many families here that are fighting, neglecting their children, withdrawing to the TV. In many cases their bright, attractive youngsters are not developing adequate character and moral standards, are failing in school, are running away, or roaming the streets as children from slum families sometimes do. So many of them are drinking too much. When I worked in a parish of poor families—many of them on welfare—I found that paraprofessionals and volunteers could often do more for families than highly-trained professionals. For example, a lower-class mother might dismiss the ideas offered by a professional social worker, saying to herself, I don't have enough education to do that sort of thing as she does. But, on the other hand, when a lower-class neighbor made the same suggestion, it would be followed; so we trained some neighborhood women who had been successful mothers to go from apartment to apartment to demonstrate better methods of child care. The visitor would read to the children, would play with them, would help parents listen to their children and try to understand them, and would invite the children to share in decisions."

He talked about a program in New York City, called the Family Union, which set out to strengthen neighborhood homes *by using and strengthening the existing self-help networks*; ethnic groups, extended families, neighborhood circles of women who traded baby-sitting or who took in food when someone was ill. They trained people in these networks to monitor and coordinate agencies and organizations that were supposed to be providing services. A neighborhood canvass, for example, found that some people were mistreated in court because they didn't understand English. They found children who were doing poorly in school because of language problems and because promised tutoring was not being provided. By persistent negotiation with agencies, or the police, or merchants, the union was able to help many families solve their problems—and keep children at home that otherwise might have been placed in foster care or institutions.

When a boy was caught smoking marijuana the union arranged for a meeting of the school principal, the guidance counselor, teachers, a psychiatrist, social workers, clergy—everyone who might be involved in a comprehensive plan to deal with the problem. The union's role was also to make sure that each agency kept its promises to the family and carried out its part of the plan. "I think we sometimes forget," the clergyman said, "how busy and pressed for time an agency official or teacher can be. We are aware of the need to keep a close eye on politicians in order to prevent graft and make sure they do their jobs right, but we forget sometimes that people in service agencies are human too. They may need prodding, or encouragement, or help from volunteers to supplement their work. When I worked in the slum I naïvely thought that we had all the family problems, that out here in the suburbs the same services and guidance were not needed to nurture and to improve family life. But I now realize how fragile our families are in American society. Once they were strong, were rooted in faith and patriotism, holding their values proudly and supporting each other. The healing and reconciling of their children after punishment was accomplished in a context that does not exist anymore. Now we must work at it more deliberately."

One-Person Supplementary Families?

Danny's psychiatrist said, "There may be no way to create networks for some isolated families and youngsters. Half the families in the country may soon be one parent with one child. I wish the clubs and churches in this community would develop an 'adopted-aunt-and-uncle' program as well as the adoptive 'grandmother program' which is emerging in one of the senior-citizen's clubs here." He pointed out that Jack Horn ("Hidden Factors in Violent Families," *Psychology Today,* December, 1978) found that child abuse is more common among people who lack sustaining interpersonal relationships, that "parents who share family decisions are less likely to be abusive." Many youngsters, tempted to run away, will go to the home of an older friend or relative if they have such a place to go. But as training is needed for parents and foster parents, so the volunteer aunt needs help to get the skills which, for example, Downey Side provides for the baby-sitter-counselors which go into the home to supervise troubled youngsters when parents must be gone. Popular magazines and scholarly journals report an increasing variety of experiments to provide relationships for youngsters like the Big Brothers-Big Sisters program. People in neighborhoods are beginning to realize that they can and must help provide such relationships for all youngsters, even if only until more effective services are provided.

The young sociologist who has been involved with Emilio proposes what he calls the one-to-one substitute family. Jerome Miller, president of the National Center for Action on Institutions and Alternatives, reported a similar experiment in the *New York Times,* June 30, 1978: In Massachusetts persons were being hired from the community—with a full-time salary to look after one youngster. It cost about one-sixth over against keeping a juvenile at the Spofford Detention Home. "The state could save a lot of money," Luiz said, "employing unemployed young Ph.D.'s like me—psychologists and teachers who can't get jobs—and who would rather devote full time to a juvenile criminal than drive a taxicab for a living."

"Turn Emilio over to me," he continued, "and I would feed him, clothe him, educate him, counsel him, know where he is all the time. I would devote whatever energy was necessary to finding him a job, tutoring him in schoolwork, supervising him, and sticking with him as an "uncle" until he was well established in life. Maybe a paid professional relationship isn't the best alternative, but it would be better than jail where Emilio is learning to be dependent, alienated, and not how to get along outside. Did you read in the newspaper about the convict who refused to leave prison because he knew no one outside? He had not even received a letter or Christmas card for years. Even as an unpaid volunteer I am Emilio's best hope. Without me he has little chance for a place in society when he comes out, after his punishment is finished." Volunteers could at least provide a one-person family.

Judge Lisa Richette in *The Throwaway Children* (New York: Dell, 1969) suggested the need for a "new type of guardian for vulnerable children," perhaps similar to the European system of "affiliation"—a procedure halfway between outright adoption and court wardship. Churches and community organizations can recruit and train people to establish warm, sustaining relationships with youngsters whose families are failing them. Many efforts are underway to improve the quality of training of foster parents, for example. The Pennsylvania State Foster Parent Association advocates a "citizen review system"—local boards to keep an eye on all foster homes. They also support revision of the state law to mandate periodic review of all children in foster homes. In addition to services to "sandbag homes," communities may next need to mandate periodic review of the homes of all children who are continually delinquent or involved in crimes.

CHAPTER 15

Jobs

THE RECONCILIATION of the juvenile after punishment essential to its completion and effectiveness requires job training and a job. "This country is going to have a serious juvenile crime problem," Lena's Vista worker said, "until we find meaningful employment for every kid who wants to work." The 1975 California strategy for delinquency prevention proposes that it is essential to "... *strengthen attachment of young people to society* by enhancing the community's capacity to provide a participating stake in societal institutions for all youth." A stake in society can include active involvement in sports, community organizations, and politics; but essentially it means work which will make it possible to buy property or save money to marry. "Youngsters in Lena's community do not take their schoolwork seriously but they take their criminal activity seriously because there are no jobs available to them with the skills provided by the schools. Crime is often the only path of life which society offers them," Miss Eleanor said.

"Yet," she continued, "look at this neighborhood. There is enough work needed here for an army! Everything needs painting, repairing, cleaning. In Switzerland when there weren't enough jobs for youngsters, the government employed them to plant flowers everywhere, to put flower boxes on the docks, in the windows of every public building, to make Swiss cities into lovely and pleasant places to live and to attract tourists and other businesses."

The long-range solution to juvenile crime must involve programs to provide jobs for all juveniles who need money because a nation which fails to do so is making crime inevitable. In the interim, however, there are things which neighborhoods and volunteers can do. Lena's community now has a Dial-A-Teen program manned largely by church volunteers to help youngsters find odd jobs: window washing, mowing lawns, cleaning yards. Block organization tag sales are raising funds to employ youngsters to do such work for the elderly and the sick who lack funds to pay—and to clean up the yards of negligent absentee owners. For a time this effort was supplemented by what the Vista worker called the "job-sharing program." A group of high-school boys from a more prosperous neighborhood, tired of having their bicycles and sports gear stolen, formed a "corporation" to solicit jobs which they shared—each working as a partner with a boy from Lena's project. With some publicity their corporation was able to increase the number of odd jobs available, especially from church members in the city.

Monitoring Job Programs

Jobs which were funded federally for youngsters from welfare families were diverted to the children of politicians in some cases, and to other neighborhoods than Lena's in others. A young Puerto Rican policeman, asked about post-punishment reconciliation in Emilio's neighborhood, pointed to the Spanish Pentecostal Church: "I've never been very religious," he said, "but when I was assigned to work with juveniles in this high-crime area I soon learned that the most effective force here is not the police department. The people in that church," he said, "the most indigenous of all neighborhood organizations, were more able than anyone else to see that the politicians did not neglect the neighborhood." Senator Moynihan in his book, *Maximum Feasible Misunderstanding* (New York: Free Press, 1969), also pointed to the street-oriented, storefront churches as providing—along with some labor unions and other small organizations—the stake which people need in neighborhoods like Lena's and Emilio's to make them responsible citizens, the "new foundation for people's lives."

The young policeman spoke of what happened when city hall got money from Washington for programs to divert juveniles from crime. "They brought in outsiders," he said, "as they always do, instead of cooperating with the Spanish church and other existing groups." He described how the outsiders poked fun at the high moral standards of the Pentecostal young people and set up competing programs to try to lure them away from the church instead of working to reach the pimps, prostitutes, addicts, and thieves, which was their assignment. "Not because of separation of church and state," the policeman went on, "but because those outsiders were only here to advance their own careers and it would have been much too hard work for them to reach the real criminal juveniles. They gave lip service to building up community organizations which could 'empower residents politically to demand jobs for our kids'. But they really did nothing for the youngsters at all."

The result? After the "poverty money" from Washington was spent, the outside political appointees left and the organizations they had started all collapsed. "All that remains is the Spanish church, with its large numbers of young people organized to help each other. Now that the Washington appointees are gone the young people on the street are even more cynical about politics and more crime-prone as a result of their cynicism for the system. With some support from people in suburban churches and organizations we could develop a much more effective job-training program through the church."

"We?" I asked.

The young policeman grinned. "Sure, I joined the church because I care about the kids on the street and there is no other organization really able to penetrate the juvenile networks." A Downey Side parent had said to me, "Few fathers and mothers have adequate skill to use peer pressure, and the adolescent networks which set the mood, the standards of acceptable behavior and dress, and through which the kids counsel each other—often badly. But formal counseling at school or elsewhere has a hard time competing with the advice that kids give to each other. If a youngster is in a criminal network, it is almost inevitable that he will commit crimes with his friends, unless you get him out of it or change the network. Families and neighborhoods become helpless to deal with juveniles unless they know how to monitor these drug, music, sport, or other networks. It takes an investment of time on the part of parents, volunteers, and neighborhood leaders to get in touch with and use these networks." Lena's criminal organization began as such a network, but after the cycle of crime and arrest had been redirected through the Vista workers into a constructive volunteer job program, Lena and also other youngsters were given a more responsible stake in the community. The young policeman in Emilio's neighborhood, saddened by the despair of youngsters he was assigned to work with on the street, saw such help by volunteers in neighborhood organization as the only hope.

Voluntary Jobs

Lena's effective reconciliation after her punishment has been possible because of the block and neighborhood organization which has challenged her passionate interest in lieu of a paying job—which she has been unable to find. She had earlier been excited about plans to rebuild her neighborhood—the original federally-funded redevelopment plan which had called for parks, playgrounds, a cultural center, and rehabilitated homes and buildings.

"I cried sometimes," she said, "when I walked down my old street to see how it looked, with yards full of garbage, abandoned houses set on fire preventing the neighbors from getting insurance." She was echoing the words of her Vista worker when she said, "What we most need here to keep kids out of trouble is organization so the residents can control what goes on in it, can run the government programs themselves." Money was appropriated for a drug dependence center, a youth center, and a health center in Lena's neighborhood, which were supposed to require "constructive involvement of residents," but the funds were frequently wasted without the residents ever really being consulted. And much of the money was actually diverted elsewhere. Jobs and job training that were intended for young people from Lena's project were dissipated in "planning" at city hall.

Miss Eleanor, the Vista worker, said, "I would create a 'ward council' with representatives from each block organization and from all the churches and indigenous organizations. Such a council, with heavy involvement by the kids, would decide how all program funds are to be spent. Instead of Lena's pastor going on hands and knees to city hall to beg for funds that were already allocated for the drug program here, I would have the city-hall politicians come here to ask for their share. My organization would have a youth council responsible for neighborhood rules, for hearing grievances, for placing representative young people on every organization which has any responsibility for jobs and job training."

The Task Force on Juvenile Justice of the Ohio Council of Churches proposed in 1977 a collaborative system for dealing with youth crime which included the formation of "neighborhood assemblies." They saw the need for "mobilization of neighborhoods into accountable components of the total community structure." The task force asked for training programs to qualify volunteers to help youth in developing "gratifying roles in political life," including participation in assigning police to neighborhoods. Lena's Vista worker and her pastor have had lengthy discussions with young people in the crime-prone project to ask them what to do to reduce crime. That task force has more recently called for a program of "urban rangers"—on the model of rangers in national and city parks—which would be assigned to city blocks. The ranger, a person skilled in supervising and training youngsters, would be assigned to work with young residents painting, repairing, and beautifying their own blocks. He would supervise and enable restitution when ordered by the court or when youngsters themselves decided to restore what they had damaged. He would need funds to employ any youngster who needed money and was willing to work for it. He would provide close supervision for all youngsters on his block, somewhat like that which the concierge provides for every apartment house in France—or which a caretaker provides for a suburban estate.

"But wouldn't this take large amounts of tax money?" I asked.

"Maybe a foundation or church will help us experiment with one block to demonstrate what might be possible. It wouldn't have to be terribly expensive, if we could persuade police, teachers, and social workers to move into the block to help."

Lena's pastor was skeptical, "Police refused once before to live in the project. They said it wasn't a safe place for their children. The police union threatened to strike if the city tried to force any of them to move back from the suburbs into the project or any other such place here. The police aren't willing to let their families live here since it is a dangerous place for children."

Miss Eleanor laughed. "This project has the largest percentage of children of any neighborhood in the county. If it isn't safe for the children of a policeman, because of our 'flood of juvenile crime'—then shouldn't we prepare to evacuate all the children immediately? Isn't that what we do when there's a flood that makes a neighborhood unsafe?"

The *Washington Monthly,* September, 1977, suggested that young people must learn the arts of politics and self-government on the neighborhood level if American freedom and democracy are to survive. Allen Lind, in the *Futurist,* December, 1975, says that the trust which people must have in government and law will in the future require small-scale networks and loyalties, which added together will constitute the larger fabric of society. *Agenda For a City* (Sage Publications, 1970) described how "district councils" might set local priorities, could act as local housing authorities, could enable neighborhood citizens to control their lives through small manageable units of government. And Senator Moynihan of New York, tongue-in-cheek, once pointed out that Castro in Cuba solved the problem of juvenile crime by giving machine guns to the delinquents—by which he meant giving them adult responsibility and political power. Can they get their jobs any other way?

From St. Matthew 17: "Lord have mercy on my son . . . I brought him to your disciples *and they could not help him.*"

And Jesus answered: "O faithless and perverse generation, how long am I to be with you? How long am I to bear with you? Bring him to me . . . I say to you, if you have faith as a grain of mustard seed you will say to the mountain: Move! . . . and it will move; *and nothing will be impossible for you.*"

By the way, if you would like to meet Jimby to ask what he thinks about a "lady judge who knows how to *punish well*," look around your hospital emergency room for a young guy whose boss says, "We're delighted to have Jimby as a full-time employee now. Our only complaint is that he works too hard and won't go home at the end of his shift if there's anyone here who really needs help."

Acknowledgements

In addition to many people who cannot be named because of confidential information they supplied, special appreciation is here expressed to: Dr. Richard Walker, Research Psychologist at the Gesell Institute; The Rev. Norma Everist, Faculty of Wartburg Theological Seminary; Robert Forsberg of the New Haven education support project; and Mayor Frank Logue of New Haven, for helping with access to materials; Susan Hathaway, Connecticut Department of Adult Probation; Dr. David Duncombe, Yale Medical School; Dr. Sonya Hoffman, former inner-city teacher; Dr. Oliver Schroeder, Director, Law-Medicine Center, Case Western Reserve University; to many others who have read and criticized the manuscript, including Dr. Richard Otto, my wife, Jean, who for ten years was reading consultant in an inner-city high school; and to my editor, Ingalill Hjelm.

Appreciation should also be expressed to friends at St. Mary's Greek Orthodox monastery where this book was outlined, to the *Christian Century*, where some of it was published; and to Dr. Garnet O. Adams, and others who invited me to lecture and develop some of this material at the Tenth Annual Conference on Children and Youth for Eastern Pennsylvania social workers, clergy, youth leaders, and school counselors for the International Year of the Child, at Womelsdorf, Pa., in May, 1979.

Recommended for Further Study

Chapter 1 — On court punishments see: J. Ardenaes, *Punishment and Deterrence* (Ann Arbor: University of Michigan Press, 1974); Steven Box, *Deviance, Reality, and Society* (London: Holt, Rinehart, and Winston, 1971); J. Cedarbloom et al., *Justice and Punishment* (Bloomington: Indiana University Press, 1971) including a recommended essay by C.S. Lewis; Michel Foucault, *Discipline and Punishment* (New York: Pantheon, 1978); J.F. Short, ed., *Delinquency, Crime, and Society* (Chicago: University of Chicago Press, 1978); Charles Silberman, *Criminal Violence, Criminal Justice* (New York: Random House, 1978); J.Q. Wilson, *Thinking About Crime* (New York: Basic Books, 1975); F.E. Zimring et al., *Deterrence* (Chicago: University of Chicago Press, 1973).

Chapter 2 — For the evidence of history on the failure of harsh punishment alone to prevent juvenile crime — when young offenders were drowned, enslaved, maimed, burned, hanged at age nine, starved, tortured, see: Eugene McCarthy, *America Revisited* (New York: Doubleday, 1978); and Wiley Sanders, *Juvenile Offenders for a Thousand Years* (Chapel Hill: University of North Carolina Press, 1970).

Chapter 3 — Morton Hunt, *The Mugging* (New York: NAL, 1972), detailed study of a mugging case, shows how "less punishment" could have prevented the further criminal career of a young mugger. See also Arnold Rubin, *The Youngest Outlaws: Runaways in America* (New York: Messner, 1976).

Chapter 4 — Nat Hentoff, "Some of Our Children Are Dying" (*Saturday Review*, Jan. 11, 1977); Howard James, *The Little Victims* (New York: David McKay, 1975), on "impossible jobs" given to teachers, social workers, welfare personnel, and others.

Chapter 5 — Episcopal Canon Clinton R. Jones, *Homosexuality and Counseling* (Philadelphia: Fortress Press, 1974); E.M. Schur, *Crimes Without Victims* (New York: Prentice Hall, 1965); L. W. Sherman, *Scandal and Reform: Controlling Police Corruption* (Berkeley: University of California Press, 1978).

Chapter 6 — Marilyn Walsh, *The Fence* (Westport: Greenwood, 1976), on the adults who make stealing profitable for youngsters.

Chapter 7 — John Holt, *Escape from Childhood* (New York: Dutton, 1974); Sara Davidson, "To Treat a Disturbed Person Treat His Family" (*New York Times Magazine,* Aug. 16, 1979).

Chapter 8 — Patricia Sullivan (*Psychology Today,* Oct., 1976) reports research through school records and interviews to investigate a similar schoolboy suicide after undiagnosed reading disability and unjust arrest. Brutal abuse of teen-age inmates like Wisher is further documented in Susan Fisher, "Life in a Children's Detention Center" (*American Journal of Orthopsychiatry,* April, 1972); (*New York Times,* Feb. 19, 1978).

Chapter 9 — H. H. Marshall, "The Effects of Punishment on Children" (*Journal of Genetic Psychology,* 1965), pp. 106, 133; William Glasser, *The Identity Society* (New York: Harper and Row, 1975), on alternatives to punishment. On theology of reconciliation, see A. Ritschl, *The Christian Doctrine of Justification and Reconciliation* (Edinburgh: T. & T. Clark, 1900); Sir Walter Moberly, *Responsibility* (London: Oxford University Press, 1951).

Chapter 10 — Samuel Yochelson and Stanton Samenow, *The Criminal Personality* and *The Treatment Process* (New York: Aaronson, 1976 and 1977).

Chapter 11 — D. Ward et al., "Videopolitics, Videotape and the Law" (*Intellect,* April, 1975); M. Garber, "Neighborhood Based Child Welfare" (*Child Welfare,* February, 1975).

Chapter 12 — Kenneth Wooden, *Weeping in the Playtime of Others: America's Incarcerated Children* (New York: McGraw Hill, 1976); Charles Hampden-Turner, *Sane Asylum* (New York: Morrow, 1977).

Chapter 13 — Dr. Lawrence Weed, *Implementing the Problem-Oriented Medical Record* (New York: Medical Communications Press, 1976).

Chapter 14 — Kenneth Keniston and the Carnegie Council on Children, *All Our Children: The American Family Under Pressure*

(New York: Harcourt Brace Jovanovich, 1977); on Downey Side see Paul Strasburg, *Violent Delinquents* (New York: Monarch 1978); and Parker Rossman, "Adopting Teenagers: The Solution for Delinquency" (*Christian Century*, December 27, 1978).

Chapter 15—Oscar Newman, *Defensible Space: Crime Prevention Through Urban Design* (New York: Macmillan, 1973); on jobs: Daniel Schreiber, ed., *The Profile of the School Dropout* (New York: Vintage, 1968).